What people have said about the works of Corvis Nocturnum

On *Embracing the Darkness; Understanding Dark Subcultures*:

"A poignant and introspective voyage into dark subcultures with a humanistic approach...a must-have for anyone who has ever wondered what draws us to the dark side." ~ Dark Realms Magazine review of *Embracing The Darkness; Understanding Dark Subcultures*.

I0160404

On *A Mirror Darkly*:

"Corvis Nocturnum delves into the dark side with clarity and vision." ~ Reverend Shane Bugbee, Radio Free Satan.

Promethean Flame reviews:

"*Promethean Flame* traces varied threads of free-thinking as practiced by rampant individualists, sorcerers, rogues, and creators as well as secret societies, also touching upon how their inextinguishable sparks continue to impact our contemporary culture in both cinema and music. It will kindle your desire to delve even more deeply into these fascinating people."
~ Magus Peter H. Gilmore, High Priest, Church of Satan

"*Promethean Flame* is an excellent study into particular developments of magickal practice and esoteric spirituality. With determination, the author blends well-researched information about key figures known for their involvement in free-thinking magickal spirituality, and examines occult orders from ancient times to modernity, even illuminating significant concepts by linking historical details to modern cinema! From John Dee to Isaac Newton; from the Golden Dawn to the Illuminati; from Zeus to Baphomet, Promethean Flame documents a wide array of history pertinent to anyone immersing themselves in the magickal arts, be they a Hermeticist, Ceremonial magician, Witch, or esotericist."

~ Raven Digitalis

Author: Goth Craft: The Magickal Side of Dark Culture

(Llewellyn, 2007)

Promethean Flame
by Corvis Nocturnum

Acknowledgments

The author would like to thank the following people for their inspiration and encouraging the celebration of rationality ...

Johann Goethe, Hegel, Richard Wilhelm Wagner, Martin Heidegger, Eliphas Levi, Thomas Paine, R. Green, Partha Bose, Helen Ellerbe, Carl G. Jung, Voltaire (both past and present day satirists), Aristotle, Plato, Socrates, and a multitude of The Decadent Romantics such as Mary and Percy Shelly, Poe, and Lord Byron, Magus Anton LaVey, Friedrich Nietzsche, Ayn Rand, P.T. Barnum, H.L. Mencken and the endless list of others...

Very special thanks to the following for editing and previewing thoughts; Starr, Cindi Petit, Magus Peter H. Gilmore, Raven Digitalis, Michelle Belanger, Paul Trimble, Adam Jackson and Timothy Ringenberg, without all of whom I would not have done this work justice. Your patience, thoughts, and hours of delightful conversation were instrumental to the completion of this work.

Dedication

In memory of my great-grandfather and grandfather, both Masons. In addition, to my grandmother, who loved the occult, the paranormal, and all of the creative arts.

To contact the author, please refer to his official website:
www.corvisnocturnum.com

Or send an SASE to:
P.O. Box 11496, Fort Wayne, Indiana 46858-1496

Other works by author include:
Artwork inside of Julie Strain's Nightmare on Pinup Street (Heavy Metal, 2004) under the name of DarkartistV

Embracing the Darkness; Understanding Dark Subcultures, (Dark Moon, 2005)

A Mirror Darkly, (Dark Moon Press, 2006)
ISBN: 978-0-6152-4257-6

TABLE OF CONTENTS

Introduction

According to ancient myth, the Titan Prometheus was the creator of man. Under orders of Zeus, he populated the world with all sorts of creatures, and endowed them with gifts such as claws, fur and wings. However, in taking so long in constructing a creature in a shape after the gods themselves, the various gifts had been depleted on the others by the time he got to man. Prometheus felt sorry for the mortals he saw shivering in the cold winter nights, so after arguing with Zeus to aid them, all to no avail, he decided to take fire from Olympus. After stealing Apollo's chariot, he carried a burning fennel stalk to a group of humans and bequeathed its secrets to all humankind. In order to placate the Father of Gods, Prometheus killed a great bull then served it to the Gods. However, always the trickster he in fact served them only the bones, gristle and fat, and feasted upon the meat with his human friends, further incurring the wrath of Zeus. Zeus punished him for this and various other crimes.

The story of Prometheus is very similar to those of Loki from Norse tales, also a giant instead of a god. Both were tricksters and associated with fire, and incidentally, both were tortured while chained to a rock for disobeying their supreme god. The Promethean myth also bears a close resemblance to the fall of man in the Judeo-Christian tradition. The gift of fire can be equated with the forbidden fruit. Ironically, the name Lucifer literally translates to "Light Bearer," hinting at a borrowed concept of the stolen fire from heaven. After looking closer at various myths of the world it is clear that in each we see aspects of the vengefulness, jealousy, and repression of humanity by Zeus, Odin and Yahweh that are identical with each other.

The work contained within this book is a greatly detailed history of rebellion against such dogma and repression. From various accused heretics, I trace the lineage of questioning Christians to modern day occultists, new age spirituality, and LeVey's Satanism. Outlined are the basic thoughts and actions from noted figures such as Grandmaster Jacques De' Molay, John Dee, Sir Francis Bacon, Eliphas Levi, and Aleister Crowley, to philosophers ranging from Johann Goethe, Friedrich Nietzsche, Martin Heidegger, Herbert Spencer, H.L. Mencken, and Ayn Rand.

I allege that, despite the Gnostic-Cabbalistic beginnings which strove with altruistic benevolence for the betterment for the goodwill of all humankind; these principals became the bedrock of future for more self-serving and rational elitists. Predominantly through time freethinking scientists, artisans, romantic period authors, and occultists questioned all things in order to attain the truth.

It is this Promethean quality of determination against all else that lights our way. I wish you all good journey out of the darkness by passing on the torch as you follow the paths of those before us.

Corvis Nocturnum

Chapter One

Esoteric and the Occult

Defining Esoteric and the Occult

Both esoteric ideas and elements of ritual in the occult have long been perceived as evil or forbidden. The very meaning of the word esoteric can be found in Webster's Dictionary as follows: "*adjective* Etymology: Late Latin *esotericus,* from Greek *esOterikos,* **1 a** : designed for or understood by the specially initiated alone <a body of *esoteric* legal doctrine" or "**b** : requiring or exhibiting knowledge that is restricted to a small group **2 a** : limited to a small circle <engaging in *esoteric* pursuits> **b** : <an *esoteric* purpose> **3** : of special, rare, or unusual interest occult means." Moreover, occult is derived from Latin *occultare,* frequentative of *occulere*: to shut off from view or exposure."

This hidden knowledge has expressed itself in a multitude of ways. In our current times, we are immersed in ancient and 'heretical' concepts. The Dark Ages and Renaissance thinkers may nearly be forgotten to all but scholars, but the Promethean rebels of its day and after have lead us to where we are today, in a world we have grown into as a society that we all take for granted.

As the young Romantic philosopher Schelling said, "The analogy of each part of the universe to the whole is such that the same idea is reflected constantly from whole to part and part to whole. The analogies of the different parts of physical nature among themselves serve to establish the supreme law of creation, variety in unity, and unity in variety. What is more astonishing, for example, than the relation of sounds and forms, of sounds and colors?"

These words left their impression on countless other writers, from Baudelaire to Ralph Waldo Emerson. If those who would have shackled our freethinking ancestors had instead allowed them to remain unchallenged, the world as we know it would not exist. We live as well as we do because all things connect, one simply has to open their eyes. We find as far back as Pythagoras with his mathematical equations the probabilities and geometry for sigils in magic and building. Without scientific territories and the contributions of aboriginal shaman to apothecaries, we would not have pharmaceuticals today, or doctors. Without builders and architects of Hiram and later his Masonic followers, we would not have monuments of our species - from the great Pyramids to the modern marvels today across the globe, to Leonardo Da Vinci who influenced the Wright Brothers with his flying apparatus. We see fact and fiction merging in wild tales by the likes of Jules Verne in his *20,000 Leagues Under the Sea* in which the *Nautilus* was extrapolated from French submarine designs during his day. This visionary pushed the ideas farther than any before him, as so often happens in our world, fantasy one day becomes reality – what the mind can conceive another can build.

Promethean Flame traces the two aspects of this rich complexity in a two fold way. In part one we look at esoteric orders shrouded in mystery and key figures in history, such as Napoleon and America's Founding Fathers, to Wicca's founder Gerald Gardner and Aleister Crowley, both in the middle of the 20th century. In the second part, we examine philosophy, literature and other arts and artisans ranging from Aristotle to Beethoven and Mary Shelley. Such outstanding men and women shook our worldview and contributed to our reshaping of man's destiny. By the end, it should be clear that the two parts have not only intersected, but could not exist without each other.

In every society, we find congregations of people. The use of symbols, signs and passwords are all around us. It is all part and parcel of communication. Membership in religions, secretive or not, is an amalgam of aspects of everyday life. They have objectives and importance beyond the mere scope of the group, into the outside world. Public opinion may be the opposite of their true intent, whether from ignorance, bigotry or fear. Their actions and beliefs have a wide range in goals, as does any organization. Intent is the key here – pillars of communities were aligned to Masonic ideals, Deists, and Illuminati schools of thought, bringing western civilization to what it is today due to the various concepts in the past. Just as Christianity was illegal in Rome in its infancy, so too were other large groups of thinkers after them, being

7

deemed a dangerous innovation. The wheel of suspicion, mistrust and hate continues, and only the faces and ideas change. It is due to that repetition that this trend continues in a variety of ways. Due to this cycle fear of groups and the power large bodies of like minds can produce, it is no small wonder that secret societies perpetuate incorrect speculation. Most followers, we will find, wanted to better the self through education, expansion of the literary arts and quite often assisted in the eventual betterment of society via governmental changes. From a sociological point of view, it is clearly an obvious requirement for progress.

Let us begin our journey into this mystery by starting in one of civilization's birthplaces, the Middle East.

Old Man of the Mountain

Nearly every one you talk to knows of the old man of the mountain – the wise old sage who imparts advice to seekers of knowledge. Few however, know the details of this. Ancient wisdom does indeed stem from this nearly mythic figure; however, Hassan was hardly a kindly old man. Those familiar with Chaos Magick might know that it is the summary of the philosophy of Hassan I Sabbah. According to Hassan, 'Nothing is True. All is Permitted' (from the Principia Discordia). Discordianism itself is a bit tongue-in-cheek in and of itself, as most wise sayings go, tending to impart wisdom with a mock serious nature.

Promethean Flame by Corvis Nocturnum
Chaos Magic

In Chaos Magick, there exists no one or correct way to achieve an effect; whatever works is what you go with, and what works changes from moment to moment. Hassan was also quoted, in the same book, as saying, "Everything is True. All is Permitted," which merely reinforces the idea. If it works, it must have been correct.

Typically, Chaos Magick is applied over another system; it simply makes the original system more malleable. Wiccans begin bending their rules, attempting strange effects, and above all, listening to their inner voices. Basically, one is attempting to 'go with the flow' to allow the self to become guided by the universe, and let the universe (a Chaos construct) take care of itself (and, as a component of the universe, you). Order is temporary at best, and typically delusional at worse.

This brings us to Discordianism, and the philosophy of Chaos. Beginning with Hassan's wisdom, we discover another interesting affect; the more you try to control a thing, the more chaotic things become. There is a continuous struggle between those who attempt to create order, and those who resist. The more order applied, the greater the likelihood of revolt. The more disorder, the more likely controls are enforced. These are the opposing forces and the spark that drives the universe, according to Discordianism. This is the sacred Chao, comprised of the opposing forces of Hodge (order), and Podge (disorder). The whole Discordian ideology is in itself a bit tongue in cheek, so to speak, but some of the Chaos theories floating around need be clarified and how it evolved from Hassan. Discordians simply attempt to manipulate these opposing forces to create effects they desire, feel are worthwhile, or help advance whatever side of the issue they are feeling closest to that day. All of this either is the application of, or re-enforced by, the Chaos Theory. And when someone mentions "Hodge podge" to you, now you know were it came from!

Chaos Theory is actually a collective set of theories, which include the "butterfly effect," (the basis of the movie with that same name, starring Ashton Kutcher). This theory is that a small change, in one system result in a massive change in another, seemingly unrelated system, a ripple effect. The other theories are The Anthropoid Principle (the universe seems to exist in such a manner to allow for the evolution of beings which could observe that the universe seems to exist), and the Observation Principle (a natural system is effected by the expectations of the person observing it-especially in quantum mechanics, where particles behave based upon the expectations of the observers, in some cases appearing before their existence, etc). Chaos Theory(ies) provides scientific backing for the philosophical and mystical applications, in and of itself making these applications more likely to succeed. Chaos Theory is actually less involved with true chaos, and more involved in attempting to discover the underlying pattern, no matter how obscure, in seemingly random events. Chaos persons typically relate to God forces such as Coyote or Eris, and are often engaged in projects designed to remind the casual observer that a) they are being controlled or forced to conform, and b) they still have the freedom to resist. Such projects have included events like the Dada Art Movement, large helium balloons being hung along a section of a well-traveled highway, and social engineering pranks (like using super strength epoxy to seal shut the coin-slots of vending machines). The effort is designed to disrupt the static paradigm of reality to allow for more potential; the more people that recognize the limits of the system, the more limited the system becomes. The movie *Fight Club* proposed multiple layers of both social engineering and Chaos ideas. In challenging our way of viewing wealth and basic human urges to vent rage (pent up anger in daily 'normal' life) the central character felt the levels of rich versus poor needed to be leveled – by leveling a building housing credit card records with explosives! The alter ego of the main character, played by Brad Pitt, used anarchy and violence to show how controllable people could be, his control over them was so absolute to the point they would not obey his orders even if they conflicted with his own prime directives. In this manner, we see the control Hassan had over his own men, as well as both Hodge and Podge used in a modern example.

The Assassins of Hassan sects killed with impunity, brainwashed as any cultist are, to obey without questioning the right or wrong of things. Being remorseless and without conscience, during the seventh century, fanatics of Islam divided into two groupings. One who saw Mohammed as the bringer of all divine wisdom, and the other who felt his successor more crucial to follow. The second, the Shiahs, relied on secrecy and clandestine information. In Cairo, in one of the finest universities in all Egypt, there were teachers whose hidden agenda was to create fanatics of promising students. Members of this secretive order, much like the Skull and Bones of today believed they were to receive wisdom and hidden powers. Instructors in the order were judges, military leaders of the day teaching in a similar fashion as does the Harvard secret society toady.

After nine levels of initiation, all of which were designed to mold the student with misleading information, the now trusted mentors had all the pupils firmly convinced that all religions, philosophy and the like were false.

Hassan, son of Sabbah had perfected the secret society. Rising in power with his allies, he began training his assassins.

Origins of the Assassins

The word "assassins" derived from the name Hassan, who used subterfuge, poisoned blades and undying loyalty to carry out his orders. Around the 1120's the order was exposed to the Crusaders. During the Crusades, they fought either side to further their purpose, forming a huge and powerful empire. Even Richard the Lionheart had been accused of killing a rival by use of the assassins. They were particularly useful as allies in taking Baghdad and other cities. It was during this time the Knights Templar came into knowledge previously unknown to Europeans on a good deal of subjects, nearly eradicated during previous years, such as philosophy and science.

Promethean Flame by Corvis Nocturnum

Typically, the members of the Order of Assassins wore a white tunic with red sash. I have no doubt that they greatly influenced the Templars in more than dress, but in the conception of secret societies as a whole. Both the Knights Templar and later the Hospitallers borrowed many of Hassan's rites and rituals to their system of initiation. Even the degree "Grand Master" terminology comes from the Order.

History of the Templar

The Seal of the Knights depicting the two riders upon one horse has been interpreted as a sign of poverty or the duality of both monk and soldier. The Knights prided themselves on the fact they were so poor but loyal they would ride two to a horse if need be. The largest and most powerful of the Christian military orders, the Poor Knights of Christ and the Temple of Solomon, originally named The Poor Knights of Christ and the Temple in Jerusalem is widely known as the Knights Templar. They were founded in 1118, in the aftermath of the First Crusade of 1096, in order to help the new Kingdom of Jerusalem maintain itself against the hostility of its Muslim neighbors, and to ensure the safety of the large numbers of European pilgrims who flowed towards Jerusalem after its conquest. The Templar Knights were identifiable by their white surcoat with distinct red cross emblazoned above the heart or on the chest, as seen in many portrayals of crusading knights in the 2006 film *Kingdom of Heaven*, starring Orlando Bloom. It is speculated they felt John the Baptist was more crucial to their thinking than Jesus was.

The Templars were well connected and quickly became embroiled in politics of the Crusades period. Organized as a monastic order, they followed rules created for them by Bernard of Clairvaux, French monastic reformer and political figure. Widely known for his piety and mysticism, he was instrumental in the in rallying support for the Second Crusade. Bernard believed the Knights were doing God's will, feeling instead they were not committing homicide, but ridding the world of evil. A large portion of the public at first distrusted the order, for the teachings of Jesus was a message of love, peace, and patience. They could not fathom the odd combination of monk and soldier together.

In time, they were granted several extraordinary Papal bulls less commonly known as *Omne Datum Optimum*, which permitted them to levy taxes and accept tithing in the areas under their direct control. This most definitely facilitated their quick rise to institutional power.

There were four divisions of brothers in the Templars: the knights, equipped as heavy cavalry; the sergeants, equipped as light cavalry and drawn from a lower social class than the Knights; the farmers, who administered the property of the Order; and the chaplains, who were ordained priests and saw to the spiritual needs of the Order.

At any time, each knight had ten people in support positions. Some brothers were devoted solely to banking, as the Order was often trusted with precious goods by participants in the Crusades. As such, they became one of the first highly structured military of its kind. The majority of the Knights Templar trained for warfare, being primarily a military order directly responsible only to the Pope. Some consider the Knights Templar to be the forerunner of the modern professional mercenaries and elite Special Forces units. The Templars used their wealth to construct numerous fortifications throughout the Holy Land and were probably the most disciplined fighting units of their Day.

The Templars' historical headquarters was on the Mount. What the Templars thought was the Jewish Temple of Jerusalem, was in fact the Dome of the Rock, an Islamic shrine on the summit of Mount Moriah, which they renamed Templum Domini, which translates to "Temple of the Lord." This summit is sacred to both the Jews and Christians as the Temple Mount as well as to Muslims as the Noble Sanctuary. The Templum Domini later became the model for many subsequent Templar churches such as the Temple Church in London, as well as represented on several Templar seals.

The headquarters of the Templars in Portugal was in the Convento de Cristo. Templars were given extensive possessions including castles in newly discovered land.

When members joined the order, they often donated large amounts of cash or property to the order since all had to take oaths of poverty. Combined with massive grants from the Pope, their financial power was assured from the beginning. Since the Templars kept cash in all their chapter houses and temples, it was natural that in 1135 the Order started lending money to Spanish pilgrims who wanted to travel to the Holy Land. The Knights' involvement in banking grew over time into a new basis for money, as Templars became increasingly involved in banking activities. One indication of their powerful political connections is that the Templars' involvement was usury, which usually meant charging a fee for changing money. The charge was typically sidestepped, by a stipulation that the Templars retained the rights to the production of mortgaged property. It is rumored that the Swiss banks were begun by the Templars, as hinted at in the *Da Vinci Code* by Dan Brown.

Over time political connections and awareness of the essentially urban and commercial nature of the Outremer communities naturally led the Order to a position of significant power, both in Europe and in the Holy Land. Their success attracted the concern of many other orders and eventually that of the nobility and monarchs of Europe as well, who were at this time seeking to monopolize control of money and banking after a long chaotic period in which civil society, especially the Church and its lay orders, had dominated financial activities. The Templars' holdings were extensive both in Europe and in the Middle East, including for a time the entire island of Cyprus. The term 'haughty as a Templar' is an ironic twist of fate from their meager beginnings when the once poor knight that had to ride two to a horse according to the legend and seal depicts. Commoners who once used the Templars as guards in their pilgrimage to Jerusalem began to despise them.

The fall of the Templars may have started over the matter of a loan. Philip IV, King of France needed cash for his wars and asked the Templars for money. They refused. The King tried to get the Pope to excommunicate the Templars for this but Pope Boniface VIII refused. Philip sent his councilor, Guillaume de Nogaret, in a plot to kidnap the Pope. Boniface VIII died only a month later from shock due to the attempt and ill treatment. The next Pope, Benedict XI, lifted an excommunication on Philip IV but refused to absolve de Nogaret. The next Pope, Clement V, agreed to Philip IV's demands about the Templars, and later moved the papacy to Avignon. This is described in *The Da Vinci Code*, where the segments of the Bible began being argued, to keep or discard truths or manipulate the followers best. Higher members in the Templars must have realized some changes were coming, as seventeen ships disappeared on October 12th, bearing away a vast fortune to parts unknown. On October 13, 1307, all the Knights Templar in France were simultaneously arrested by agents of Philip the Fair. Seeing the fate of the Templars, the Hospitallers of St John of Jerusalem, of Rhodes, and of Malta were also convinced to give up banking at this time. The Pope transferred much of the Templar property outside of France to the Knights Hospitaller, and many surviving Templars were accepted into the Hospitallers. The Knights Hospitallers, members of the military and religious Order of the Hospital of St. John of Jerusalem, who were sometimes called the Knights of St. John and the Knights of Jerusalem. The symbol of the Order of St. John came to be a white cross-worn on a black robe; thus, the Hospitallers were the Knights of the White Cross, in contradistinction to the Knights Templars, the Knights of the Red Cross. The Maltese cross was put to use by various secret organizations, which have been falsely alleged to have a connection with the Knights of St. John., including The Knights of Malta. The cross with eight points was used long before the Maltese by many Crusaders, each point of the arms representing eight virtues. Malta became the fixed home of the Order and gave its name to the knights. Meanwhile, the Protestant Reformation had dealt a severe blow to the order. It refused to yield to Henry VIII in England, and the English branch was suppressed. In Malta, the order continued to live in fear of the Turks, with whom they fought in 1565. The hospital at Malta was the equal of any in Europe, and the knights continued their charitable work. There was some reorganization of the order, and admission became more and more a test of nobility of birth.

The order received its deathblow when Napoleon Bonaparte on his Egyptian campaign took Malta in 1798. We'll learn more about Napoleon's love/hate relationship with the Masons later on. The knights were compelled to leave, choosing Czar Paul of Russia as Grand Master by an illegal election, which was later validated. Many of the Knights went to St. Petersburg but with a Roman Catholic Order and the permission of the Pope, passed under the rule of an Orthodox emperor and by this time the order was practically at its end. In 1879, the Pope restored the office of grand master, but the reconstructed order that resulted has very little relation to the old Knights of Malta. It is a charitable organization especially devoted to the care of the sick that has continued to expand considerably over the centuries, and as we see now have an association in the United States.

Many kings and nobles supported the Knights at the time of the Crusades, and only dissolved the order in their fiefs when so commanded by Pope Clement V.

The dominant, and probably more accurate, view is that Philip, who seized the treasury and broke up the monastic banking system, was jealous of the Templars' wealth and power, because it is believed he owed a substantial sum of money to members of the Knights and sought to control it for him. These events, and the Templars' original banking of assets for suddenly mobile depositors, were two of many shifts towards a system of military fiat (a decree of payment, servitude or barter) to back European money, removing this power from Church orders. Allegations of demonic activity on the Knights' part arose when Philip IV plotted along with Clement V to destroy the order.

Philip IV had Grand Master Jacques de Molay and 140 other Knights arrested in the Paris Temple. Soon, more arrests followed through-out France.

Claims of heresy

Debate continues as to whether the accusation of religious heresy had merit by the standards of the time. Some argue these accusations were, in reality, due to a misunderstanding of arcane rituals held behind closed doors. They were charged with idol worship – of a decapitated head. This head has often been referred to as Baphomet, about which I'll go into more depth on later. Supposedly, additional crimes included denying Christ and spitting on the Cross three times, as well as kissing other men's buttocks – this is an accusation among witches later for "kissing Satan's arse." As well, they were charged with heresy in trying to synchronize Christianity with Islam. Some scholars argue that the former referred to rituals involving the alleged relics of Saint Euphemia, one of Saint Ursula's eleven maidens, Hughes de Payens, and John the Baptist rather than pagan idols. During the judicial proceedings and inquisitions of the Knights Templar, assertions were made that the Knights engaged in pagan idolatry. This led them, under torture en masse for months, to admitting to heresy in the Order. Members of the order admitted to renouncing the Nazarene and spitting on, trampling and urinating on the crucifix. Among other accusations were charges that the Knights were engaging in intercourse with demons, indulging in all manner of "sexual perversity" and worshipping the idol of Baphomet.

Statements had been obtained from former Knights stating that the Order secretly worshipped an entity they called Baphomet. There was secrecy surrounding the Templars meetings and wild rumors spread concerning bizarre initiation rituals that did much to promote public suspicion of the order. Of course, due to such secrecy, accusations flew rampantly – the outsiders upset by the power and wealth of the Templars, the Roman Catholic Church with its inquisitors accused them of Devil worship, blasphemy, sodomy, and idolatry. According to *The Di Vinci Code* by Dan Brown (which has been turned into a film by the same name starring Tom Hanks) it was due to the fact Jesus was human and not a demigod and the Grail was the womb of Mary Magdalene. Regardless of whether this was truth or entertaining fiction based on various historical facts, it would have been a deathblow to the power structure of the patriarchal church. These confessions were obtained under duress and were later recanted; therefore, their validity is highly questionable.

Baphomet

Baphomet appears in many contemporary works of horror and fantasy fiction. H.R. Giger's bio-mechanical interpretations of Baphomet in his art in the mid 1970's as it appears in his first hardback book as well as the 2007

Levi's illustration

21

calendar depict a very accurate version, paying homage to Levi's illustration.

The most common and famous illustration was given to the world by the classical occultist, Eliphas Levi, and it first appeared in his work *Rituel Et Dogme De La Haute Magie*. Levi believed that Baphomet was symbolic of the Astral Light, which has roots in primordial matter. Levi was also insistent that there was a correlation between Baphomet and Pan. A recent film, *Pan's Labyrinth* depicts the best version on the silver screen I've ever had the pleasure to see, and certainly mixes aspects of both together well. Some groups of Witches invoke this being during Sabbats to strengthen the link between themselves and the web of life. Baphomet is the All begetter and All devourer, merging man, animal and plant, and it is ever changing, ever growing and dying. It is mindless, only filled with a Dionysian will to grow, feed, mate, survive and die, repeatedly. It is filled with the ecstatic joy of life and death, and exists inside every living being. The purpose for the invocations that the Witches and magicians do is to awaken this force and set it free.

Baphomet is usually depicted as a demon (per Levi's interpretation,) but often is depicted as a hermaphrodite. This Templar idol has been variously described as having a human skull for a head, as I found, having two faces, as a cat-like creature or alternately as a bearded head. The head worshipped by the Templars has been made mention on a History Channel show, after the popularity of *The Da Vinci Code* craze hit. Sometimes it was thought to be a Goddess although we may never know. In his book, *Supremely Abominable Crimes*, author Edman Burman presents the following information: "A head with one face or two faces, sometimes bearded and sometimes not, made of silver or of wood, a picture of a man or of a woman, an embalmed head that glowed in the dark or a demon."

The idol was said to be the source of fertility and wealth. Baphomet makes a rare film appearance in the 1968 Hammer Horror film *The Devil Rides Out*. Baphomet is one of many demons popularly referenced in black metal music and related artwork, such as in the lyrics of the English band Venom and the American band Goatwhore.

We see many unique demons or monsters named Baphomet appear in computer and video games. *Doom II* and its sequel have at their final levels a creature alternately called "Baphomet" or the "Icon of Sin". The plot of the video game *Broken Sword: The Shadow of the Templars* involves a sect of Templars that worships Baphomet. He is a demonic patron in "In Nomine." Usually this figure is described as a monstrous head, a demon in the form of a goat, a figure with the head of a goat and the body of a man, and was thought to symbolize the burden of matter from which arose the repentance for sin. The human hands formed a sign of esotericism to impress mystery upon the initiates and represented the sanctity of labor. Two lunar crescents, the upper being white and the lower black, represented good and evil, mercy and justice.

The lower part of the goat's body was veiled but expressed the mysteries; the universal generation is symbolized by the phallus. Being hermaphroditic, the female breasts were the symbols of maternity, toil, and of redemption.

Baphomet was affiliated with many great occultists and organizations over the centuries; The Knights' Templar, Levi, in works by Aleister Crowley, and Anton LaVey and his Church of Satan to name a few. Each person generally has his or her own personal opinion of what Baphomet represented. The Knights of the Templar looked upon the skull of Baphomet as being symbolic of personal wealth, and fertility. Other than the goat's skull within the inverted pentagram, the other most common depiction of Baphomet is the illustration of the goat-headed man perching on a platform on tarot cards and sundry other illustrations.

The worship of Baphomet has survived since time immemorial, having been worshipped by the cult of Mendes in Egypt and the Bacchants of ancient Greece. The worship survived in some mystery cults during the Classic Period, and well into the Middle Ages. Some of the myths about Witches Sabbaths may well be distorted legends about the cult of Baphomet. Today magicians are actively interacting with Baphomet, and by invoking and worshipping Baphomet, they feel one may gain insight into the secrets of life, and feel its power. Baphomet is the sum of all life, and knows all its secrets and desires.

Levi called his image "the Baphomet of Mendes." He combined the images of the Tarot Devil card and the he-goat worshipped in the city of Mendes. It is unclear whether the Ancient Egyptian women had intercourse with the goat during religious rites for fertility, but the Catholic Church claimed this and it is possible that this is where the notion that the Devil had intercourse with witches came from. The goat or ram was used as the master of fertility and was celebrated as "copulator in Anep and inseminator in the district of Mendes," where women were blessed with children. During rituals, women danced naked before the image.

Levi's depiction, for all its fame, is not particularly authentic to the historical description from the Templar trials, although it is not unlike gargoyles found on several Templar and non Templar churches— or the vivid gargoyles added to Notre Dame de Paris about the same time as his illustration.

This "Sabbatic Goat" may have partially derived from the 18th-19th century Spanish artist Francisco Goya, who painted a "Witch's Sabbath" in 1800 in which a group of seated women were offering their dead infant children to a seated goat.

Different theories exist as to the origin of the term, including from the Greek words 'Baphe' and 'Metis'. The two words together would mean "Baptism of Wisdom". A certain Dr. Hugh Schonfield, a scholar who worked on the Dead Sea Scrolls, believed that the word "Baphomet" was created with knowledge of the Atbash substitution cipher, which substitutes the first letter of the Hebrew alphabet for the last, the second for the second last, and so on. "Baphomet" rendered in Hebrew, after interpretation, becomes the Greek word "Sophia", or wisdom.

Satanists from the Church of Satan, use Baphomet as the name of their identifying sigil, a point-down pentagram enclosing a goat's head, surrounded by five Hebrew letters spelling out

"Leviathan". The Hebrew letters at each of the points of the pentagram starting from the lowest point and reading counter-clockwise. Translated, this is Leviathan, a sea creature figuring in Judaic mythology. Leviathan is commonly associated with Satan, and the fourth book of *The Satanic Bible* is named the Book of Leviathan.

According to Magus Anton LaVey, Baphomet was one of the infernal names used as a key to call upon dark forces, saying that He delighted in committing blasphemy against the Golden

Dawn Magicians "Satanifying" the angelic beings. He then divided *The Satanic Bible* into corresponding parts to the elements and crown princes of Hell as he felt appropriate. Baphomet was symbolic of indulgence, a force, which can be summoned by mages, but it cannot be easily controlled. Although versions of the Sigil of Baphomet appear as early as the 1897 book *"La Clef de la Magie Noire"* by Stanislas de Guaita, the variant in common circulation today was designed for use by the Church of Satan, and is known as the Sigil of Baphomet. This variant is copyrighted by the Church of Satan and cannot legally be reproduced without permission.

This could very well be basis for the Egyptian- Templar-Masonic and Crowley connection, which is my conclusion after researching the timeline of everything for this book. Historically Baphomet is thought to symbolize the burden of matter from which arose the repentance for sin. Of course, Crowleyites still maintain Baphomet is one of the names of their master, Edward Alexander "Aleister" Crowley, whose notorious character garnered him attention in the 20th century. Crowley did sign many documents with this name, as well as other fanciful handles, such as "To Mega Therion", which is Greek for "The Great Beast". Crowley did not accept his contemporary, Eliphas Levi's, version of the evil-looking Baphomet as the object of the anti-Knights Templar accusations with Harpocrates, the Ram of Mendes. However, for the 16th major trump card of Crowley's tarot deck, we find it depicts the Ram standing beneath a stylized phallus, as a friendly four-legged, multi-eyed animal-god, not a demonic half-human hermaphrodite.

A slanderous deformation of the Latinized "Mahomet", a Medieval Latin rendering of Muhammad - the name of the prophet of Islam is a possible explanation of the name of Baphomet being altered over time. During the era of the Crusades, European literature contained considerable misinformation and distortions against Islam and its prophet, such as the claim that Muslims worshipped a god called "Termagant". It is therefore possible that the name "Baphomet" represents one more such incident, and was coined by the enemies of Islam, and made deliberately to resemble "Mahomet" for propaganda purposes. The interaction between the Templars and Muslims during the course of the Order's history would make the charge of secret Islamic idolatry very plausible for the time. Christian writers typically equated all anti-Christian beliefs with idol worship and devil worship. Idries Shah, writing as "Arkon Daraul" in his book about *Secret Societies*, has proposed that "Baphomet" may actually derive from the Arabic word Abufihamat, meaning "The Father of Understanding". Wherein he states, "Probably relying on contemporary Eastern sources, Western scholars have recently concluded that 'Baphomet' has no connection with Mohammed but could well be a corruption of the Arabic "Abufihamat"). The word means 'father of understanding'. In Arabic, 'father' is taken to mean 'source, chief seat of,' and so on."

Promethean Flame by Corvis Nocturnum

Levi proposed that the name was composed from a series of abbreviations: 'Temp. ohp. Abi.' that originates from Latin 'Templi omnium hominum pacis abhas,' meaning "the father of universal peace among men." An alternative reading could be tem. o. h. p. ab. for templi omnium hominum pacis abbas. The translation in this case is abbot of the temple of peace of all mankind, perhaps referring to the Templars themselves, feeling Solomon Temple's purpose was to bring peace to the world. This, we will find, is a shared concept of both Masons and the Rosicrucians. Baphomet as an archetype has survived since time immemorial.

Suppression of the Knights Templar often goes far beyond the suggested motive of seizing property and consolidating Theo political power. At the same time, it is the Catholic Church's position that the persecution was unjust, that there was nothing wrong with the Templars, and that the Pope at the time was manipulated into suppressing them. The church's response at the time corroborates this position. The Papal process started by Pope Clement V, to investigate both the Order as a whole and its members individually, found virtually no Knights guilty of heresy outside of France. Fifty-four knights were executed in France by French authorities as relapsed heretics after denying their original testimonies before the Papal commission; these executions were motivated by Philip's desire to prevent any more Templars from having similar courageous ideas. It failed miserably, as many others testified against the charges of heresy in the ensuing Papal investigation.

In the end, the only three accused of heresy directly by the Papal commission were Grand Master of the Knights Templar Jacques de Molay and his two immediate subordinates; they were to renounce their heresy publicly. Molay regained his courage and proclaimed the orders and his own innocence; along with one of his companions The Papal commission found that the Order as well as Clement V, however, fact growing public opinion against the order, felt that the only choice was to suppress it. It should be noted that Clement V by no means co-operated willingly with Philip was the passing of the majority of the Order's wealth and lands to the Hospitaller order, although Philip and other European nobility held some Templar lands for many years in contradiction to Philip's wishes that he appropriate their wealth in France.

Jacques de Molay's curse

Legend has it that as de Molay, after being imprisoned and tortured for seven years, was burned alive at the stake- at which point he cursed King Philip and Pope Clement V to meet eternal justice within the year. Pope Clement V died only one month later and Philip IV seven months after that. Commentators were extremely pleased with such a development and often featured this story in their chronicles. The little known fact that day of October 13, 1314, "Friday the thirteenth" is attributed with bad luck began on this particular day in history. It certainly was for the Templars, and the same pattern would again repeat itself time and again.

The Knights Templar was but the first of many who would find themselves at odds with the Roman Catholic Church. We will see next how divisions in the minds of others in the coming centuries would aid in the evolution of Europe and in America into what it is today.

Chapter Two

Rosicrucian Society

While taking a look at occultism and the rebellious nature of men away from the Church, it may be odd to think that Christian were also the center of attention by the Papacy, but in those Days any deviation was considered heretical. Masons and The Rosicrucians both were viewed as traitors against the strictness of the iron fist of the Holy Roman Church. Thus, the following chapters focus on the key groups and persons who began the path away from dogmatic thinking. I tend to think of these Christian Pagans as ancestors to the truly free and liberated magicians of later years; without the basic ideas and dictations questioned, progress would not have been possible to the advancements we have today.

Much after the Templars suppression, rumor continued that secret societies thrived on into The Middle Ages. Sufi Masonry returned to Europe from the Middle East. The Church had turned its attention towards witchcraft, largely due to The Inquisition, instigated during 1484 by the publication known as *The Malleus Maleficarum* by Dominican monks Heinrich Kramer and James Sprenger. The authors of "The Witches Hammer," as it translates to, are one of the primary reasons occult practitioners remained hidden. Despite Christian ideology mixed heavily into practitioners of Masonic Templars and the like, fear kept them silent. Prior to the Inquisition, pagan worship of gods and goddesses went unobstructed by the Church, considered a non-important practice of "delusioned lost souls in the countryside." Pope Innocent VIII's paranoia continued the vendetta against anything not sanctioned by the Church, as did his predecessor Clemet the V.

Jewish mysteries known as the Cabbala came to Europe in the 1550's and were mixed with Gnosticism and Heretic philosophy, eventually becoming known as the Golden Dawn. We will explore this in greater detail later on. The major book on Hermetics, *Corpus Hereticum*2 fell into the Medici family's hands.

The Medicis

The Medicis were a powerful and very influential Florentine family during the 13th through the 17th century. The family was known to patronize the arts, and allegations were made that many of the artists and scientists whose works they encouraged had Pagan or occult influences, despite the fact that three members of the family were Popes; Leo X, Clemet VII, and Leo XI. The Medicis financed the translation of rare magical texts into the modern language. The wealth they amassed through the Medici Bank helped begin the Italian Renaissance. For a period of time they were the richest family of all Europe, and beginning in

─────────────────

2 *Corpus Hermeticum*, which was basically a body of works attributed to Hermes, god of herbology, occultism, and medicine have been formed for the study of Rosicrucianism and allied subject

Florence they widened their leverage that, which held for decades over most of the civilized nations. The family generously bequeathed vast sums to the arts, lending their patronage to Donatello and Michelangelo, as well as to art galleries and gardens all over Florence. They were patrons to Galileo, the famous scientist who taught their children and was an important figurehead for his patron's quest for power. Ferdinando II eventually abandoned Galileo's patronage when the Inquisition accused Galileo of heresy. However, the Medici family did afford the scientist a safe haven for many years. In a move to gain the support of the family Galileo named the four largest moons of Jupiter after four Medici children that he tutored. During a time when his works were both sought after by kings and feared by the Church, a few world famous scientists saved themselves by using schemes Machiavelli would have been proud of.

Niccolo Machiavelli

Niccolo Machiavelli was a Florentine political philosopher, born May of 1469. This oft-misquoted man was a musician, poet, and romantic comedic playwright. He was a very good friend of Leonardo Da Vinci also.

Machiavelli was also a key figure in realist political theory, crucial to European statecraft, during the Renaissance. Machiavellianism is the term some social and personality psychologists use to describe a person's tendency to deceive and manipulate others for personal gain. This term is also used to describe later works by other authors based on Machiavelli's writings – particularly *The Prince* written in 1513– in which the authors stress the view that I find he was a key figure in reshaping how we make decisions, as it is often said "the end justifies the means," however he did not make that exact statement. This phrase, more accurately known as Consequentialism, is a moral philosophy. *The Prince* contains no equivalent phrase, and the idea of that phrase goes back further in written history to Plato at around 360 BC. This type of moral philosophy has evolved to encompass ideas such as Marxism and Fascism, in which the head of state carries out the moral philosophy on a societal and various levels of social life. It is a phrase has that has evolved encompassing two beliefs, including that morally wrong actions are sometimes necessary to achieve morally right outcomes, and that actions can only be considered morally right or wrong by virtue of the outcome. In reverse, people who believe that the consequences of any immoral action are greater than those of the expected outcome will often say that the ends *do not* justify the means. These authors failed to include some of the more moderating themes found in Machiavelli's works and the name is now associated with this extreme viewpoint. Machiavelli died in June of 1527.

This revival of Paganism, in writing along with Classical cherubic artworks of the Renaissance, flourished due to artists such as Leonardo Da Vinci and writers like Milton. *Treasures in the Louvre* and texts of *Faust* today would not have been made into classics without the advent of the Medicis. We'll discuss art, literature and philosophy in other chapters in great detail.

Christian Rosenkreutz

According to a legend published in the 17th century Rosicrucian manifestos, a German pilgrim named Christian Rosenkreutz, who studied in the Middle East under various occult masters, founded the Rosicrucian Order in 1407 (the early 15th century). I find it a touch amusing the founder was named Christian! During his lifetime, the Order was alleged to be small, consisting of no more than eight members. When Rosenkreutz died in 1484, the Order disappeared, only to be "reborn" in the early 17th century. Most modern Rosicrucians accept this legend to varying degrees. Some accept it as literal truth, others see it as a parable, and yet others believe Rosenkreutz to be a pseudonym for a more famous historical figure, usually Francis Bacon, a man whose contribution to esoteric history will be further explained.

According to a lesser-known legend found in Masonic literature, the Rosicrucian Order was created in year 46 when an Alexandrian Gnostic sage named Ormus and his six followers were converted by one of Jesus' disciples, Mark. From this conversion, Rosicrucianism was born by fusing early Christianity with Egyptian mysteries. By this account, Rosenkreutz, rather than being its founder, would have been initiated into and become the Grand Master of an already existing Order.

According to Émile Dantinne, the origins of the Rosicrucians may have an Islamic connection. As told in their first manifesto *Fama Fraternitatis* (early 17th century) Christian Rosenkreutz started his pilgrimage at the age of sixteen. This led him to Arabia, Egypt and Morocco, where he was put into contact with the sages of the East, who revealed to him the universal harmonic science. After learning Arabic philosophy in Jerusalem, he was led to Damcar. This place remains a mystery. It did not become Damascus, but it is somewhere not too far from Jerusalem. He then went to distant lands in Egypt, where he did not stay for long. Soon afterwards, he embarked on a quest to expand his understanding of philosophical and occultist studies, such as alchemy, astrology, magic, and esoteric science. However, Dantinne states that Rosenkreutz may have found his secrets amongst the "Brethren of Purity," a society of philosophers that had formed in Iraq during the first half of the fourth century. Their doctrine had its source in the study of the ancient Greek philosophers, but it became more pronounced in a neo-Pythagorean direction, as I will explain later on. They adopted the Pythagorean tradition of envisioning objects and ideas in terms of their numeric aspects. Theurgy taught the divine and angelic names, conjurations, the Quabalah, exorcisms, and other related subjects, an influence on philosopher John Dee.

Before this time, great works considered heretical were destroyed in great number, the backlash of the ignorance that resulted in the Dark Ages. It is a fact that other countries salvaged copies of classics by Greek and Roman scholars, which in turn were copied, or obtained them from secret society members, and strongly influenced "new" thoughts during the Renaissance. These works, having been rescued, lead to an exodus from the bleak period that fanatics in the Church would have plunged all of the old and New World into.

The "Brethren of Purity" and the Sufis are similar in many points of doctrine. Both were mystical orders deriving from Koranic theology, with the dogmatic faith in the "Divine Reality." Many similarities with the Rosicrucian way were expressed in the manifestos as well as the "Brethren of Purity" ways of life as well. Neither group wore special clothing, both practiced abstinence, healed the sick, and they offered their teachings free of charge, having taken an oath of secrecy never to reveal their origins. The metaphorical quality of these legends lends to the nebulous nature of the origins of Rosicrucianism. For example, the opening of Rosenkreutz' tomb was considered only a way of referring to the cycles in nature and to cosmic events.

It is on the foundation of these teachings that Rosenkreutz conceived the plan for simultaneous and universal religious, philosophic, scientific, political, and artistic reform. For the realization of this plan, he united with several disciples (seven at first, according to *Fama Fraternitatis*), to whom he gave the name of Rose-Croix. The founder of the Order of the Rose-Croix belonged, as affirmed by historians, to a noble family, but there is no document that allows us to affirm this peremptorily. A number of isolated individuals became what now is known as "The fraternity of the Rose Cross." Like the Masons, they held certain views in common: hermetic knowledge related to the higher nature of man, and philosophical conceptions aimed towards the foundation of a more perfect human society. It is evident that the writers who posed as Rosicrucians were moral and religious reformers, and utilized the technicalities of chemistry, or more specifically, alchemy. Their writings included a hint of mysticism or occultism, promoting inquiry and suggesting hidden meanings discernible only by "Adepts."

The Rosicrucian's rose appears in *The Da Vinci Code* as well, detailed on a wooden box containing a puzzle, which kept leading to other clues.

Leonardo Da Vinci

When one hears the words "Renaissance Man," most likely they refer to Da Vinci. Leonardo Da Vinci was born in Tuscany, near Florence, were he flourished. The handsome and brilliant youth was a persuasive conversationalist who became an apprentice to Andrea Del, a sculptor and painter.

Although few paintings of his still remain, he is most famous for his painting of the *Mona Lisa*, *The Last Supper*, and *The Vitruvian*

Man. The hype of the film named after the inventor became so big Marvel Comics has even redone this ancient sketch of man in multiple poses using Spider Man, in the same parchment and sepia style art on a t-shirt.

During the infancy of engineering Da Vinci conceived ideas far beyond his time. Animals such as birds and turtles inspired his drawings of the first glider like plane, a tank and submarines – complete with a double hull. His notes, though many were either lost or destroyed as blasphemy, greatly advanced metallurgy, anatomy, and civil engineering. Duke of Milan, who attempted to hold back the French in 1495, employed Leonardo as a military thinker. In Florence, he entered the service of Cesare Borgia, the son of Pope Alexander VI, where he designed ramparts and defenses, as well as enormous catapults, and began his tank design. He developed multiple row cannons that having been fired would rotate on a wheel for another row to reappear and fire again – the first machine gun. He thought up cluster bombs, despite the fact he personally felt war was one of humanity's worst activities. In his heart, he was a pacifist.

For a while, he lived in Rome, but after peace talks with Pope Leo X and France settled disputes, the French King Francois the First hired him. Giving him a large sum of money, the king was said to have commented to an artist named Benevenuto Cellini the he believed Da Vinci was a man who, unlike any other who had ever lived, had *"learned as much about sculpture, painting, and architecture, but still more that he was a very great philosopher."*

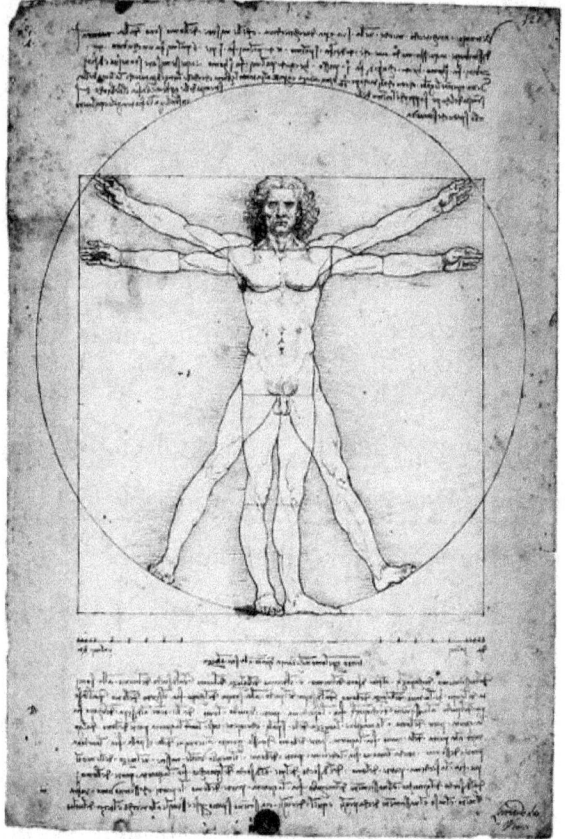

Here again, I note that free thinking in the spirit of Prometheus existed in one of the most time revered men. As were many rebels like him both before and after, Leonardo Da Vinci was eccentric. His feats include using a mirror to pen his notebooks so that the writing was difficult to understand, and remarkably, he could draw with one hand while writing with the other! Da Vinci taught himself Latin, despite not having any formal education, and because of that fact, most scholars during his time ignored him. Leonardo dissected thirty corpses at an Italian hospital, gaining a vast understanding of anatomy, which he coupled with his artistic understanding and knowledge of anatomy to invent, had due to the fact he had. He was the first to detail the human spinal column as "s" shaped, and also did drawings of a fetus in the womb and x-ray styled depictions of humans having sex. It was his hope to be the first person to draw a human appendix. Making nearly 200 drawings, his work, no doubt, has assisted both artists and medical students over time. His findings on the human heart inspired British surgeons to pioneer new ways to repair hearts in the year 2005. He built what is now known as Leonardo's Robots, a fully armored knight that could stand or sit by use of internal pulleys and wheels. An episode of the History Channel detailed many of Da Vinci's works, showing art and, with computer animations showed the workings of the robot and first tank. One of the few surviving books, called *The Codex Leicester* written by Da Vinci now is owned by Bill Gates, who displays it once a year in different cities around the world.

His view on sexual anatomy, expressed that was that 'the act of procreation and anything that has any relation to it is so disgusting that human beings would soon die out if there were no pretty faces and sensuous dispositions,' was later interpreted by Sigmund Freud, in an analysis of the artist, as indicative of his "frigidity." Around 1476, while still living with Verrocchio, his lover, he was accused anonymously of sodomy with a 17 year-old model, Jacopo Saltarelli, a youth already known to the authorities for his sexual escapades with men. After two months of investigation he was acquitted, due to the fact no witnesses stepped forward though some claimed it was due to his father's respected position. In *The Book of Dreams*, a fictional dialogue on *l'amore masculino* (male love) written by the contemporary art critic and theorist Gian Paolo Lomazzo, Leonardo appears as one of the protagonists and declares, 'Know that male love is exclusively the product of virtue which, joining men together with the diverse affections of friendship, makes it so that from a tender age they would enter into the manly one as more stalwart friends.' It is a much talked about fact Da Vinci had a thirty year relationship with a man named Salaino despite the fact Salino was a stubborn liar and thief. The handsome adolescent was depicted in a few of Da Vinci's notebooks. A priest destroyed many of the artist's erotic drawings, depicting sexual intercourse, after Da Vinci's death. Count Melizi, an aristocrat he met in 1506, is said to be Leonardo's life mate. Leonardo, Melzi and Salaino traveled together through out Italy for some time.

Leonardo Da Vinci died at Clos Luce on May 2, 1519. As he wished, 60 beggars followed his casket to the chapel of the Amboise castle. Da Vinci left the world far more advanced than it was during his own time. Perhaps it is through the lifetime of work of Da Vinci and others, that we are now where we should have been a long time ago, despite the Dark Ages.

Promethean Flame by Corvis Nocturnum
Chymical Wedding

From 1614 through 1616, the publications of *Fama Fraternitatis Rosae Crucis*, *Confessio Fraternitatis*, and *Chymical Wedding of Christian Rosenkreutz* caused immense excitement throughout much of Europe. These works declared the existence of a secret brotherhood of alchemists and sages who were interpreted as preparing to transform the artistic, scientific, religious, political, and intellectual landscapes of Europe while wars of politics and religion ran rampant across the continent. All three documents probably were the creation of Lutheran theologian Johann Valentin Andréa. However, his authorship which had only has been confirmed for the *Chymical Wedding*. The authors of the Rosicrucian works generally favored Lutheranism as opposed to Roman Catholicism. Largely in secret hopes that splintering the Church into more and more denominations would weaken the might of their largest opposition.

Around the year 1530, well over eighty years before the publication of the first manifesto, documented evidence of the cross and the rose already existed in Portugal in the Convent of the Order of Christ, home of the Knights Templar, which later was renamed Order of Christ. Three bocetes (large stained glass windows) were, and still are, in the initiations room. In these cases, the rose can clearly be seen at the center of the cross. At the same time, a minor writing by Paracelsus called *Prognosticatio Eximii Doctoris Paracelsi* contained the image of a double cross over an open rose, along with a written reference to it. It is evident that the first Rosicrucian manifesto, *Fama Fraternitatis*, was influenced by the work of the respected hermetic philosopher Heinrich Khunrath of Hamburg. He was author of the *Amphitheatrum Sapientiae Aeternae*, and was, as previously mentioned, in turn, strongly influenced by the work of the mysterious philosopher and spiritual alchemist John Dee.

The legends and ideas presented in the first two manifestos and in the *"Chymical Wedding"* originated a variety of controversial issues and works of Rosicrucianists inspiration. It was erroneously thought that quite literally the members believed they could turn lead into gold. No one ever stated, in an objective way, that they had produced gold. Neither Khunrath nor any of the other Rosicrucianists ever said that they could do so; their writings point toward a symbolic and spiritual Alchemy, more than anything else does. Using both direct and veiled styles, these writings conveyed the nine stages of the transmutation of the threefold body of the human being, the threefold soul and the threefold spirit of a human being. Among other esoteric knowledge related to the "Path of Initiation". The Rosicrucian's felt turning lead into gold was a metaphorical representation of the soul perfecting itself, not an actual scientific action – with the exception of an infamous pair of rogues I'll discuss later.

The famous jewelry company Legends of England and its Gothic collection of fine pewter use Chymical Wedding as a title for a work of art on their hooded sweatshirt and various other objects. A vast number of the company's items are inspired directly by occult history, most obviously the symbols on rings and pendants, and to the shrewd observer, the base of a scrying crystal ball holder fashioned after John Dee's.

In December of 2004, daring thieves brazenly entered the Museum of the History of Medicine in London, forced open a cabinet and took the original crystal along with a note penned by Nicholas Culpeper. The remainder of affects had been transferred to the Science Museum in 1976.

The Order of the Rosary Cross

The Order of the Rosary Cross reestablished the ancient mysteries, agnostic beliefs, and healing arts. The Rosicrucian Order is a famous yet secretive Order dating from the 15th or 17th century. It generally is associated with the symbol of the Rose Cross, which is also found in certain rituals beyond "Craft" or "Blue Lodge" Freemasonry. The Rosicrucian Order is viewed among earlier and many modern Rosicrucianists as an inner worlds Order, comprised of great "Adepts." When compared to human beings, the consciousness of these Adepts is like that of demi-gods. This "College of Invisibles" is regarded as the source permanently behind the development of the Rosicrucian movement.

Several modern societies' were of a hermetic order. (The word hermetic comes from the Greek God Hermes. Occultists conflate the Greek Hermes with the Egyptian Thoth, who was also a mythological alchemist known as Hermes Trismegistus, meaning 'thrice great'.) Two books attributed to Hermes, the *Emerald Tablet* and the *Corpus Hermeticum,* where both important in connection to the Medici family. By now Italy and England were leading the way forward in science for most of Europe. Rosicrucians were believed to possess a magic ability to seal treasure chests so that nobody could access their contents. Alchemists also frequently used distillation in their experiments, and needed an airtight seal to improve the efficiency of their alembic stills. Most alchemists, though, were considered Hermetics for adopting the philosophy of the *Emerald Tablets*, a collection of nine principals on how the world works, or the *Corpus Hermeticum* having been formed for the study of Rosicrucianism and allied subjects. However, many researchers on the history of Rosicrucianism argue that modern Rosicrucians are in no sense directly derived from the "Brethren of the Rose Cross" of the 17th century. Instead, they are considered followers. Moreover, some have viewed the 17th century order as a literary hoax or prank, rather than an operative society. Others contend that history shows them to be the genesis of later operative and functional societies. Regardless of the true past, they remain a very important part of religious and occult history.

However, not all alchemists who studied the Rosicrucian ideals did so out of noble reasons – two famous scoundrels who in historically lived in the lap of luxury due to fleecing the wealthy were Cagliostro and the Comte Saint Germain. Rebels yield both good and bad; a bit of the early bad boy archetype rests in these gentlemen, no doubt.

Cagliostro

A famous alchemist (and trickster – fair to say he inspired P.T. Barnum in the expression "another sucker born every minute") was Cagliostro. He was born Giuseppe Balsamo on June 2, 1743 in Palermo, Italy. Cagliostro's father died early in his life and because his mother was unable to support him, he then was sent to live with his uncle until he ran away after which he was sent to a seminary. He ran away, yet again, from the monastery joining a band of 'vagabonds', which committed petty crimes as well as murders. Constantly in police custody thanks to his association with the vagabonds, it was only due to his uncle that he was not sent to prison for his crimes. At the age of seventeen he began studying Alchemy, and he spent years deceiving the wealthy out of precious metals, claiming he had the formula to make lead into gold. He charged a fortune in gold, promising to buy inferior metals in large quantity to change it into still larger amounts of gold.

Our charlatan Cagliostro met up with fellow trickster "the Comte de Saint Germain" in London, who initiated the eager fellow into the rites of Egyptian Freemasonry, as well as the recipes for the elixirs of Youth and Immortality. After establishing Egyptian Rite Masonic Lodges in Germany, England, and Russia as well as in France, Cagliostro settled in Paris in 1772, where he again sold medicines and elixirs and began to hold séances – a snake charmer of his day. King Louis XVI became interested in Cagliostro, and was entertained by the Count who held magic suppers for the court at Versailles. For a good many years, Cagliostro was a favorite of the court, until 1785 when he was involved in major events that led to the French Revolution in 1789. Thanks to his involvement in the scandal, Cagliostro spent six months in the Bastille and then became permanently banished from Paris.

Comte de Saint Germain

Germain is a figure of mystery, whose legend has grown in the last 200 years since his death. There are several conflicting versions of his early life, one being that he was born in 1710 in Portugal. He spoke all European languages fluently, had a complete knowledge of history, was a composer of music and was able to play the violin very well. He was most famous for his amazing skills in medicine and alchemy, supposedly for transmuting metals into gold and having a secret technique for removing flaws from diamonds. Seeing as science did not have the means to verify such claims, it is small wonder his "skills" were in such high demand.

The English writer Horace Walpole (the author of *The Castle of Otranto*, the first gothic novel) mentions his presence in London and in the English court. Saint Germain was soon expelled, having been accused of being a spy, but afterward went to France and became a favorite of Louis XV, who did indeed employ him as a spy several times. He exerted great influence over that monarch. Around 1760 Saint Germain, like his protégée, was forced to leave France and returned to England. In 1762 Saint-

Germain was found in St. Petersburg, playing a very important part in the conspiracy to make Catherine the Great Queen of Russia. A great many leaders in history were tied to secret societies, like Napoleon and infamous villains like Hitler. We'll look into these connections in detail.

Isaac Newton

Sir Isaac Newton, one of the most important geniuses of mathematics, also possessed many famous and old treatises of alchemy. He made manuscript copies of alchemical works, found today at Yale University's Library. One of these many works in his collection is the *Themis Aurea* by Michael Maier, to which he made references and comments about notes relating to hermetic philosophy.

In the 1618 manifesto, *Pia et Utilissima Admonitio de Fratribus Rosae Crucis*, he presented the concept that the Rosicrucians left to the East, due to the instability in Europe at the time of the Thirty Years' War, 1618-1648. In 1710, Samuel Ritcher also presented this idea in some of his works. However, another prominent author on the Rosicrucians arose during the same time, A.E. Waite.

It was in this fertile field of discourse, and filling the vacuum left by the original Rosicrucians, that many societies said to be "Rosicrucianists" arose. However, it is possible only a few of them may have something in common with the true Rosicrucian Order, other than the name.

According to Jean Pierre Bayard, two rites of Rosicrucian inspiration emerged from the end of 18th century. One was the Rectified Scottish Rite, which was widespread in Central Europe where there was a strong presence of the "Golden and Rosy Cross." The other was the Ancient and Accepted Scottish Rite, practiced in France. During the 18th century, there were several rites practiced in Freemasonry based on the Renaissance universe of hermeticism and alchemy, which were created by the Rosicrucians of 17th century or earlier. Although many serious research attempts were made to learn about the change from the real operative Masonry to the rumored or speculative Masonry, no concrete answer has yet been found, other than it occurred between the end of 16th century and the beginning of the 17th century.

The alchemy in the laboratory, the ancestor of modern chemistry, where the ultimate goal understood of the laws of Nature in order to aid the individual's quest for perfection, recalls another type of alchemy, the one called spiritual. The true alchemists, or philosophers of the fire, often make reference in their works to the blowers, meaning all those who were just interested in the creation of gold and the material aspects of alchemy.

In his laboratory, the alchemist works on the *materia prima* and surrounds himself, among other tools to accomplish the operations, with a furnace with a peculiar form, called an athanor.

In the point of view of Spiritual Alchemy, the *materia prima* is the human soul, and about the athanor, it is constituted by both the physical body and the subtle bodies. These last ones maintain the life of the densest one and assure the connection with the soul, or energy body. The laboratory is the human existence during which the soul has the possibility of accomplishing the learning needed to perfect itself, operating the transmutation of the vices and defects of the metal into spiritual, that is, into related virtues and qualities.

The first Rosicrucians practiced the operative alchemy, in vogue at that epoch, of interest even to the higher ranks of popes and kings. *The Chymical Wedding of Christian Rosenkreutz* is a major written work, which clearly refers, through its title, to this work on the matter, in the laboratory. Much of the jewelry created by Alchemy Gothic's (a division of Legends of England) collection is based on Rosicrucian, Templar, and Gothic churches artworks.

According to the early Manifestoes, the Rosicrucians were a "secret" Order. Their members believed or could "demonstrate" healing powers that were believed to be a gift from God: Spiritual Healing. In the outer orders these powers were explained by Egyptian mysteries and again, differently in the Order. Members were admitted on this basis alone and the "membership" was very selective. The writers, philosophers and people of the time became curious and infuriated because they were denied entrance into these secret meetings. Most of the writings of the time are biased or are very speculative for this reason. Many modern Rosicrucian organizations hold the belief that these "God given" powers may be used to help others, and other interpretations are described as being Rosicrucian. They are used as an idea or icon by persons or groups either Gnostic Christian or simultaneously Christian and trans-Christian. An example would be a cult that centers on the Virgin Mary yet openly or secretly identifies her to the Virgo constellation of the Zodiac.

A large majority of modern Rosicrucians believe in the study of Spiritual Astrology as a key to the Spirit, designed toward spiritual development and self-knowledge, as well as an aid to healing through Astro-Diagnosis. A way through which the alchemical work on the "Path of Initiation" has been expressed to the world, according to occultists such as Corinne Heline is through some of the great compositions of classical music. The nine symphonies of Beethoven (1770-1827) were divided into two groups. The first, the third, the fifth, and the seventh are vigorous, powerful and of command, representing the intellect. The second, the fourth, the sixth and the eighth are elegant, gracious and beautiful, representing the heart or intuition. They culminate in the symphony with human voices, the ninth symphony, in which the equilibrium between mind and heart or the "Chymical Wedding" ritual, where the "Christ Within" – the Adept – is born. Beethoven played a small part in the philosophy section of this work also, as I will reveal later on. Whether or not he was himself was a member of any secret society or not is still a mystery. He was however, a passionate and gifted man who hated the leaders of his day. This alone may be grounds for the rumors.

In the latter part of this work, we will discover the pagan influences in dozens of classical literature have been not only preserved, but have been touted as masterpieces by universities worldwide. We will also see that many of the works of William Shakespeare, the music-dramas of Wagner, Goethe's *Faust*, and Dante's *Divine Comedy,* and a few other books of comparable rank, are designed for esoteric as well as entertainment reading. In Shakespeare's works, specific signatures, cryptically conveyed, also are presented. *A Midsummer Nights Dream* is clearly pagan influenced, and in *Love's Labours Lost* a whole scene is devoted to revealing, in an ingenious way to those possessing the keys, the Rosicrucian connection. The scene closes with a remark addressed to Goodman Dull, a representative of the unperceiving multitude, that during the entire scene he has not spoken a word. "No," comes his response, "nor understood none neither."

If one abstracts from the symbolic associations of the rose and the cross, it is known that three treatises that gave rise to this movement became published in German between 1614 and 1616. The peak of the so-called "Rosicrucianism furor" was reached when two mysterious posters appeared on the walls of Paris within a few days of each other. The first one started with the saying "We, the Deputies of the Higher College of the Rose-Croix, do make our stay, visibly and invisibly, in this city ..." and the second one ended with the words "The thoughts attached to the real desire of the seeker will lead us to him and him to us".

The following lines can be found in *The Muses' Threnodie* by H. Adamson *"For what we do presage is riot in grosse, for we are brethren of the Rosie Crosse; We have the Mason Word and second sight, Things for to come we can foretell aright."*

The Rosicrucians took the union of the rose and the cross for their symbol because this union was a symbolic meaning of their effort and emphasizes the fact that that effort must be made by all men, as the aim of humanity on earth is to attain divine wisdom. Only two ways lead to this divine wisdom: knowledge and love. The rose blooming in the middle of the cross explains the whole meaning of the universe explained thus: in order to realize its possibilities and become perfect, humanity must develop the capacity for love to the point of loving all creatures.

John Dee

The best-known Rosicrucian in history was the philosopher to Queen Elizabeth, John Dee. He was a visionary of the British Empire; Dee coined the word Britannia. He also developed a plan for the British Navy and simultaneously trained the first great navigators. While doing so he developed many maps charting the Northeast and Northwest Passages.

Author of the Enochian keys, he was one of the first dabblers in Angelic magic. Dee was said to have conjured angels who told him what Britain would have in their eventual empire. He used an obsidian show stone that came from the Aztecs/Mayans, which now rests in the British Museum along with his conjuring table that contains the Enochian Alphabet he used as angel language. His contributions both occult and scientific to the country and the world reached far beyond his times. In addition, it is a little known fact that Shakespeare depicted Dee as King Lear.

Modern groups

During the late nineteenth and early twentieth centuries, various groups styled themselves after the Rosicrucians. Almost all claimed to be authentic heirs to a historical Rosicrucian tradition. These include the Ancient Mystical Order Rosae Crucis (AMORC), the Rosicrucian Fellowship, the Rosicrucian Order Crotona Fellowship, the Hermetic Order of the Golden Dawn, and others as well as others. These diverse groups can be divided into two categories: the Para-Masonic groups and the Esoteric Christianity groups. There has never been any connection between these two streams.

Para-Masonic groups are defined as being late heirs of the alchemy and hermetic knowledge. The inner structure of these groups is based upon Masonic lines, such as grades, initiations and titles.

The Esoteric Christianity groups regard themselves as representing a "rebirth" in the New World of the inner worlds as described by the original Rosicrucian Order. Their mission is to prepare the whole world for a new phase in Religion during the next six centuries as we move toward the Age of Aquarius.

Eliphas Levi

Born Alphonse Louis Constant in February of 1810, Levi was a French author and magician. "Eliphas Levi" was the penname, which he published his books under, was his attempt to translate or transliterate his given names "Alphonse Louis" into Hebrew. The son of a shoemaker in Paris; he attended a seminary and began to study to enter the Roman Catholic priesthood. However, while at the seminary he fell in love with a, and left without being ordained. He wrote a number of minor religious works in 1839, and later two radical tracts, *L'Evangile du Peuple* ("The Gospel of the People," 1840, and *Le Testament de la Liberté* ("The Testament of Liberty", published in the year of revolutions, 1848,which led to two brief prison sentences – quite a change of pace!

In 1854, Lévi visited England, where he met the novelist Edward Bulwer-Lytton, who was interested in Rosicrucianism as a literary theme and was the president of a minor Rosicrucian order. With Bulwer-Lytton, Lévi conceived the notion of writing a treatise on magic. This appeared in 1855 under the title *Dogme et Rituel de la Haute Magie*, and was translated into English by Arthur Edward Waite as *Transcendental Magic, Its Doctrine & Ritual*. It famous opening lines present the single essential theme of Occultism and gives some of the flavor of its atmosphere, "Behind the veil of all the hieratic and mystical allegories of ancient doctrines, behind the darkness and strange ordeals of all initiations, under the seal of all sacred writings, in the ruins of

Nineveh or Thebes, on the crumbling stones of old temples and on the blackened visage of the Assyrian or Egyptian sphinx, in the monstrous or marvelous paintings which interpret to the faithful of India the inspired pages of the Vedas, in the cryptic emblems of our old books on alchemy, in the ceremonies practiced at reception by all secret societies, there are found indications of a doctrine which is everywhere the same and everywhere carefully concealed."

I couldn't have said it better myself.

Chapter Three

Freemasonry

I have a personal reason for my fascination with Freemasonry and Modern Masons. My great grandfather and grandfather were Masons, state representatives and attorneys. So secretive typically is the membership that I did not come into this knowledge until after my grandfather's death – even my father and uncle had this fact withheld from them. It was only by finding a newspaper clipping while doing family research did I come to find out years later. It was due to my grandfathers' love of books that I, myself, became a bookworm, reading such classics as *20,000 Leagues under the Sea*, Edgar Allen Poe's *Pit and the Pendulum*, Mary Shelly's *Frankenstein* and Bram Stoker's *Dracula*. In high school I remember giving two oral book reports, on Dracula as well as one on the Crusades, all from memory, but told no one that I hadn't read them again to prepare! The works of *King Arthur* and J.R.R. Tolkien's books led me to be interested in the knights and magic, which led me down the path to the Gothic subculture, and on to study the occult and secret societies today.

There are approximately 5 million members of the Masonic Lodges worldwide, mostly in the United States and other English-speaking countries. With adherents in almost every nation where Freemasonry is not officially banned, it forms the largest secret society in the world. Freemasonry, its teachings and practices of the secret fraternal order officially known as the Free and Accepted Masons, or Ancient Free and Accepted Masons have no central Masonic authority; jurisdictions are divided among autonomous national authorities called grand lodges, and many concordant organizations of higher-degree Masons. In the both the United States and Canada, the highest authority rests with state and provincial grand lodges. Custom is the supreme authority of the order, and there are elaborate symbolic rites and ceremonies, most of which utilize the instruments of the stonemason, which are the plumb, the square, the level and compass and apocryphal events concerning the building of King Solomon's Temple for allegorical purposes.

This is the city were the goddess Isis was said to have created a replica of her husband's penis (Osiris, god of the underworld) and buried it, due to the fact Set dismembered the god's body and scattered the pieces over the world. In a temple built over the spot, it is said the worship of a goat god took place – supposed acts of bestiality took place there, with the priestess performing sex acts with goats, and the Goat of Mendes – a possible link to Baphomet's goat head.

King Solomon

Freemasonry is based upon the legend of the building of Solomon's Temple, also called the First Temple, and may have been constructed in the hidden form of a human body which is actually a composite of three biblical figures, says temple researcher Tony Badillo. The three figures are the Levitical High Priest, Jacob and a "metallic Messiah." Aztec or Mayan pyramids consist of a similar pattern, were the temple top or central ritual area is the head in design. If so, they all possibly depict a similar view: the relationship between God (the Head) and humanity (the body). Interestingly, the similarities in other temples, like the Mayan and Aztecs connections are hinted at in the film, *Alien vs Predator*. Fiction is often based on history and various faiths to make the fictional tale more believable. The measurements and description of the temple are given in the Bible. Jewish tradition tells us that Jacob (forefather of the twelve Israelite tribes) saw the Temple in advance in his dream at Bethel. After seeing angels ascending and descending on a stairway, Jacob says in Genesis 28:17, "This is none other than the house of God, and this is the gate of heaven."

The construction was said to have employed thousands of masons and stonecutters almost 3,000 years ago. King Solomon's goal was to create a glorious temple. Although he was largely viewed as Christian he accepted of pre Judeo-Christian ways, and Hiram, as well as the King of Tyre from Israel were pagan Goddess worshippers. The blending of this no doubt is the root of the Templars mixing Christianity with Islamic concepts. To the best of my research, Israel only became Christian due to relentless military campaigns. Solomon employed Tyre's temple builder and master mason, Hiram Abiff, a master artisan of wide renown, to adorn the temple and beautify it. Its design and symbols contained vast secrets beginning with the two pillars themselves, Boaz and Jachin. Occultists in the famous Tarot used these pillars symbolically. We'll find out more on this later on.

Hiram Abiff

Hiram Abiff, according to legends, was treated as an equal by the two kings. The temple took seven years to build, and seven is a significant number to Freemasonry and occult traditions. Three rogue workers were unable to extract the secrets of the Temple by force, but ended up killing Hiram. After they originally hid the body in the temple, the men then carted it away and buried it. When King Solomon was informed that Abiff was missing, he was furious and took a roll call of the craftsmen, and found three were missing. All the harbors and roads were blocked and search parties were sent out. Finally, the three were found and brought before King Solomon, to whom they confessed. Solomon ordered each of them to be executed in vile, horrific ways, with terrible torture and severing of body parts.

According to biblical tradition, the Ark of the Covenant was solemnly brought from the tent in which David had deposited it to the place prepared for it in the temple. Then Solomon ascended a platform which had been erected for him, in the sight of all the people, and lifting up his hands to heaven poured out his heart to God in prayer (1 Kings 8; 2 Chr. 6, 7). The feast of dedication, which lasted seven Days, followed by the feast of tabernacles, marked a new era in the history of Israel. On the eighth day of the feast of tabernacles, Solomon dismissed the vast assemblage of the people. Completed in the 10th century BCE, the temple was destroyed by the Babylonians in 586 BCE. According to Masonic legend, just before the completion of the temple, three rouges conspired to extract the secrets of the Master Mason's word – a belief that words had the power to invoke or destroy God's creation, the subplot to the Indiana Jones saga and other movies predate Freemasonary.

With heavy connection to modern practitioners of the Egyptian path, Crowley followers who were called Thelemites, and many others may be traced back to this time period – keep in mind that the Hebrews received their knowledge of building from the Babylonians and that slavery held its sway in Egypt – the land of gods, goddesses and symbology. An example of this can be seen from the Great Pyramids shape and with the introduction of the All-Seeing Eye's introduction to our money during Roosevelt's presidency. Roosevelt it would seem had great eagerness to have the Great Architect of the Universe placed on the back of our dollar bill. The thought of the day was that America was at a spiritual turning point, with steps to create a one-world state. This sense of worldly brotherhood in places of power is depicted in the movie *The Skulls*, implying many world leaders are a part of a blend of Masons, Illuminati, and Skull and Bones style shadow government.

Napoleon Bonaparte

Napoleon Bonaparte, also unofficially known as The Little Corporal (*Le Petit Caporal*) was one of the greatest military commanders and a risk taking gambler. He was a workaholic genius and a very impatient short-tempered man. We see a bit about him in *The Count of Monte Cristo*: a forlorn, proud and a vicious cynic who forgave his closest betrayers, yet a man who could enthrall men. Napoleon was all of these and more, the two time emperor of France whose military endeavors and raw personality dominated Europe for a decade, indeed, in thought for centuries. Although his advisor, Talleyrand, who betrayed him in the end, remains my personal favorite, (a key player in French history for his part in the greatness in the famous strategists moves.) Like Kissinger to Richard Nixon's career, little is known about the man behind other great men. Napoleon is worth mentioning here for his interaction with Masons and great challengers such as Sir Isaac Newton. When the Emperor asked a

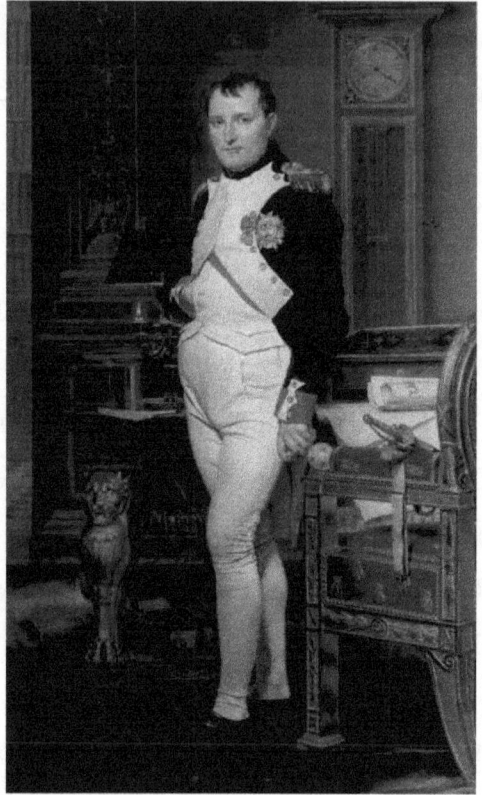

Humanist why he did not mention God in his speeches, the Humanist named Laplace, replied, "Sire, I have no need of that hypothesis." Napoleon had a strong dislike for the Masonic styled groups, as mentioned previously when The Knights of Malta were compelled to leave. Bonaparte was well aware of the Illuminati and others who were involved in the Revolution, but being rightfully paranoid, Napoleon did place some who were loyal to him in the Freemason Lodges in Paris as sources of information.

De Moley's bones and weapons were exhibited in a church with an army of Templars in knights' armor and a detachment of French soldiers. The French Masons regarded their emperor as a traitor, but then again, most of the ideals of goodwill among both Masons and Rosicrucians spurred the Illuminati to push for the overthrow of all monarchies. The same man who felt government should stay out of people's bedrooms finally decreed in 1850 that the lodges could no longer be involved in politics. The tale of Napoleon blasting off the nose of the Sphinx in target practice, in my opinion, may be connected to his dislike for Masonic history, as they were directly connected to the ancient mysteries of that land.

The ideals of this time period may have slowed to a halt in Europe, but the new American government was full of Masons and members of the Rosicrucian Order. These political changes implemented then are still in place today.

The principles of Freemasonry

The principles of Freemasonry have traditionally been liberal and democratic. Anderson's *Constitutions* (1723), the bylaws of the Grand Lodge of England, which is Freemasonry's oldest existent lodge, cites religious tolerance, loyalty to local government, and political compromise as basic to the Masonic ideal. Masons believe in a Supreme Being, use a holy book appropriate to the religion of the lodge's members, and maintain a vow of secrecy concerning the order's ceremonies. All these factors, plus the pagan overtones of the rituals, no doubt contributed to the animosity from the Church. So powerful did the Masons become, around the time of WWI and WWII, Masononic orders had become so powerful it was not permissible to be a Catholic while being a member of a lodge.

The basic unit of Freemasonry is the local Blue lodge, and is generally housed in a Masonic temple. The lodge consists of three Craft, Symbolic, or Blue Degrees: Entered

Apprentice (First Degree), Fellow Craft (Second Degree), and Master Mason (Third Degree). These gradations are meant to correspond to the three levels—apprentice, journeyman, and master—of the medieval stonemasons' guilds. The average Mason does not rise above Master Mason.

If someone does rise above Master Mason, however, he has the choice of advancing through about 100 different rites, encompassing some 1,000 higher degrees, throughout the world. In America, the two most popular rites are the Scottish and the York. The Scottish Rite awards 30 higher degrees, from Secret Master (Fourth Degree) to Sovereign Grand Inspector General (Thirty-third Degree). The York Rite awards ten degrees, from Mark Master to Order of Knights Templar, the latter being similar to a Thirty-third Degree Scottish Rite Mason.

Other important Masonic groups are the Prince Hall Grand Lodge, to which many African-American Masons belong; the Veiled Prophets of the Enchanted Realm (the "fraternal fun order for Blue Lodge Masons"); and the Ancient Arabic Order of the Nobles of the Mystic Shrine, which are Thirty-second degree Masons who, as the Shiners, are noted for their colorful parades and support of children's hospitals. There are also many subsidiary Masonic groups including the Order of the Eastern Star, of which my great-grandmother was a member which was limited to Master Masons and their female relatives; De Molay, an organization for boys; and Job's Daughters and Rainbow, two organizations for girls. Many of the Orders maintain homes for aged members.

Development of the Order

The order is thought to have arisen from the English and Scottish fraternities of practicing stonemasons and cathedral builders in the early Middle Ages. Traces of the society have been found as early as the 14th century. Because, however, some documents of the order trace the sciences of masonry and geometry from Egypt, Babylon, and Palestine to England and France, some historians of Masonry claim that the order has roots in antiquity.

The formation of the English Grand Lodge (1717) was the beginning of the widespread dissemination of speculative Freemasonry, the present fraternal order, whose membership is not limited to working stonemasons. The six lodges in 17th century England grew to about 30 by 1723. There was a parallel development in Scotland and Ireland, although some lodges remained unaffiliated and open only to practicing masons. By the end of the 18th century there were Masonic lodges in all European countries and in many other parts of the world as well.

The first lodge in the United States was founded in Philadelphia (1730); with Benjamin Franklin as a member. Many of the leaders of the American Revolution, including John Hancock and Paul Revere, were members of St. Andrew's Lodge in Boston. George Washington became a Mason in 1752. Another prominent Mason of the times was Thomas Paine.

Thomas Paine

Born January 29, 1737, this intellectual, scholar, revolutionary and idealist is widely recognized as one of the Founding Fathers of the United States. A radical pamphleteer, Paine anticipated and helped format the American Revolution through his powerful writings, most notably *Common Sense*, an incendiary pamphlet advocating independence from Great Britain. He was an advocate for classical liberalism - a philosophy shared by most of the founding fathers, resembling modern Libertarianism in its ideals of small government, personal freedom, free markets and constitutional republican government. Paine outlined his political philosophy in *The Rights of Man*, written as a general political philosophy treatise as well and, *Common Sense*, a treatise on the benefits of personal liberty and limited government, in which he considers society "a representation of human ideals, and government a necessary evil." Paine was also noteworthy for his support of deism, taking its form in his treatise on religion *The Age of Reason*. He died on June 8, 1809.

Benjamin Franklin

The most memorable image of Ben Franklin nearly every child learns in school is one of him standing in a thunderstorm

71

flying a kite, or coming up with quaint anecdotes such *as "Early to bed, early to rise, makes a man healthy, wealthy and wise."* But what they don't generally know is that he was America's first celebrity, a juvenile delinquent, a deist, and a capitalist. At the age of seventeen, he abandoned his apprenticeship to his older brother over his brother's jealousy of his ability to write for the paper the elder Franklin owned, and struck out for Philadelphia with next to little money on him. He observed his fellow man, played chess often, and studied various religions of almost every denomination. He became a skilled navigator and manipulator, which aided him later in life as a strategist among political circles. He claimed doing well was important everywhere (especially for himself). This self made man became known for starting his own newspaper (which later turned into a big business for him, by starting up other syndicated papers for a fifty percent cut), this social climber made an impression on all churches by donating vast sums of money to every church in the city. Hardly just a benevolent act, it was actually two fold ploy, to acquire a good name and it was a great public relations act to put himself in the good graces of everyone in town. He was cautious in his underhandedness, and quite the lady's man. He often remarked in his autobiography that he was amazed he never contracted syphilis from his 'lowly paid women', as he put it. He kept notes on self-improvement for himself and in others, but jokingly once said he could not expect perfection, for that would negate his goal of humility when he felt the urge to brag about overcoming his other vices!

Franklin gathered young apprentices around him for intellectual talks at a tavern, for song and drink. These comrades grew and promoted each other's careers, starting the first fire department and the first lending library. He felt that books were not the luxury of the wealthy and nobility alone, and started the first non-religious college, The Philadelphia Academy, now known as Pennsylvania University. He worked hard through his life, and made sure others saw him do so – it made him talked about. He improved our postal service during his younger years, also for ulterior motives. In turn, this made his syndicated papers immensely popular. By the time The Pennsylvania Gazette exposed the actions of English Governors, it became as influential as the New York Times during the Watergate scandal of Nixon's presidency. When he finally sold his paper, Benjamin Franklin retired at the age of 42, financially set for most of his life.

Where most people would have faded into oblivion at this time, content with the good life, Franklin was hardly finished. His fascination with science lead to the discovery of the Gulf Stream, he invented the wood burning stove named after him, and created bifocals. He worked on the phonetic alphabet, which was incorporated by *Webster's Dictionary*.

His discovery that lightning was made up of electricity staggered the world with his kite experiment, for during the early colonial times it was thought to be God's wrath on Earth. A year later in 1752, French scientists agreed with his discoveries after conducting tests a year later. He then protected buildings with lightning rods, without which we most likely would not have tall buildings today. Franklins place in history was just beginning however. After receiving many honorary degrees for his accomplishments, he added to his Humanist ideas by challenging Britain and turning against the crown. Between 1740 and 1760, he was a supporter of both the colonies and England until the Stamp Act taxation on all paper goods. England had just won the French and Indian War, which is during the time shown in the film *Last of the Mohicans*, starring Daniel Day Lewis. People loyal to England were tarred and feathered – an act which no doubt which scared Franklin, who then was still at that time for his straddling of the fence. By his pleading with Parliament, the Stamp Act was repealed.

Franklin felt compromise could be reached, even as the Boston massacre, which started the American Revolution, began. Samuel Adams requested his help, and Franklin agreed. He played rival British officials against one another, chess-like hoping to show the bad apples to the King, thinking he could get a fair shake for America. He publicized his results, and like the Pentagon Papers, it caused uproar.

The famous Boston Tea Party, Franklin again tried to play mediator in Parliament, to no avail. He went to England a British loyalist and left a Revolutionary, finally understanding that his politics were now personal. With his personality and fame, he was instrumental in getting aid from France. England, still reeling from their own war, hired the German mercenaries. We see this in the famous story of *The Headless Horseman* by Washington Irving in 1820 was recreated in the *Sleepy Hollo,* the adaptation with Goth film megastar Johnny Depp, which depicts a German mercenary soldier as the horseman, (played by none other than Christopher Walken). At seventy years old, Franklin drafted the Constitution with Adams, scratching out the word by Adams that said "hold sacred" in the second paragraph. He rewrote it to say "hold as self evident," a nod to his Humanist nature. We'll discuss Humanism in the second half of the book in more detail.

Franklin continued his jaunts from Europe to America, spending many of his later years in France. An angry John Adams was referred to as 'the other Adams" as the French thought he was Sam Adams, not John Adams. Franklin himself had such fame that Parisian women taught him French in bed, while Adams learned to speak it from books! Indeed, the reactions to his visits were closer to America's hysteria over The Beatles, Elvis or many other celebrities. Due to Franklin's connections, America leads the way for democracy even now.

During this same time period, most of the American Masonic Lodges broke away from their English and Scottish antecedents. Freemasonry has continued to be important in politics; thirteen Presidents have been Masons, and at any given time quite a large number of the members of Congress have belonged to Masonic lodges. Notable European Masons included Voltaire, composer Franz Joseph Haydn, Johann von Goethe, and many leaders of Russia's Decembrist revolt in 1825.

Because of its identification with 19th-century bourgeois liberalism, there has been much opposition to Freemasonry. The most violent in the United States was that of the Anti-Masonic party. Freemasonry's anticlerical attitude has also led to strong opposition from the Roman Catholic Church, which first expressed its anti-Masonic attitude in a bull of Pope Clement XII (1738). The Catholic Church still discourages its members from joining the order. Totalitarian states have always suppressed Freemasonry; the lodges in Italy, Austria, and Germany were forcibly eradicated under fascism and Nazism, and there are now no lodges in China.

The cutlery company Bud K Worldwide sells swords and shields emblazoned with the seals and cross. Many movies have aspects on the Templars in them, such as the Hughes Brothers' film starring Johnny Depp version of Jack the Ripper wherein it portrayed the killer as a Mason embroiled in conspiracies with England's powerful families in *From Hell*, based on a graphic novel by Alan Moore and illustrated by Eddie Campbell. The Sherlock Holmes film directed by Bob Clark titled *Murder By Decree* in 1979 incorporates Jack the Ripper and Freemasonry. (A special thanks to The Church of Satan's Magus Peter H. Gilmore for the movie reference here), and we see more details on the secrets in history of America in *National Treasure* starring Nicholas Cage. So the Templars influence our modern décor and entertainment.

The founding Fathers were largely Masons and Humanists, the details of both will be explored in each section of this book.

The Hellfire Club and Sir Francis Dashwood

The name 'Hellfire Club' conjures up all sorts of sensational and lurid images, but what was the truth behind the legend?

A group that in our current times has even found its way into the Marvel Comics 'X-Men' as aristocratic supervillians, the true and famous Hellfire Club was the organization allegedly founded by Sir Francis Dashwood (1708-1781), yet it was never called that name by its members. It was more formerly known as The Friars of St Francis of Wycombe, or The Order of Knights of West Wycombe. Dashwood was the son of a wealthy businessman who had married into the aristocracy. He sat in the House of Commons for over 20 years and variously held the offices such as Chancellor, Postmaster General and Treasurer to King George III.

As a young man, Dashwood went on the Grand Tour of Europe and enjoyed a span of time in Italy. There he fell in love with the architecture and mythology of many cultures. During this time, he developed a hatred of Catholicism, met Prince Charles Edward Stuart and became a secret agent. His hedonism and life as a spy would make James Bond envious!

Dashwood also seems to have become involved with the Rosicrucian movement through his Jacobite contacts. In Florence, he was initiated into a Masonic lodge - this event may have taken place as a result of his meeting with Prince Charles, as the pretender to the Scottish throne is known to have had extensive connections with various Masonic/Templar hidden societies. While staying in France, Dashwood also attended a Black Mass a interested spectator, although what was to become a lifelong interest in the subject appears to have been more as rebellious reaction to Catholicism than any serious attempt to practice or follow 'Satanism.' I use this term in quotes simply because in Dashwood's time, Satanism was Devil worship, not Satanism as we know it today from the 1960's.

In 1739, Dashwood returned briefly to Italy and made contact again with the Masonic societies, then went on to visit Rome during the election of the new Pope. The previous pontiff had prohibited the practice of Freemasonry in 1738 and excommunicated all Catholics known to belong to Masonic Lodges. The English Grand Master of the Florence Lodge, Lord Raynard, son of the Chief Justice of England, was forced to close the lodge down and destroy all its papers to avoid being arrested by the Inquisition. Young Dashwood by this time was no stranger to courtly intrigue or covert operations.

On his return to England, Dashwood founded the Society of the Dilettanti. This was one of many London clubs of the time patronized by the aristocracy and royalty and catering to the hard-drinking and womanizing habits of wealthy rakes.

In 1746, Dashwood founded his Order of the Knights of St Francis. They initially met at the 16th century George & Vulture public house in Cornhill in the City of London. This tavern was later to be immortalized in Charles Dickens' *Pickwick Papers.* The Knights met in a room dominated by "an everlasting Rosicrucian lamp". This was a large crystal globe encircled by a gold serpent with its tail in its mouth. The globe was crowned with a pair of silver wings and was suspended in chains in the form of twisted serpents. This lamp is not be confused with the one in the shape of a giant bat with an erect phallus formerly displayed in the Witchcraft Museum on the Isle of Man and allegedly belonging to the Hellfire Club. The Gnostic design of the Rosicrucian Lamp, incorporates a snake and doves. In 1751, Dashwood leased Medmenham Abbey on the Thames near Marlow, about 6 miles from his ancestral home at West Wycombe. It had originally been a 12th century Cistercian monastery but came into secular hands at the Reformation and was converted into a Tudor manor house. In the tradition of the 18th century Gothic revival, Dashwood converted the Abbey, at great expense, into a suitable headquarters for his Order, installing stained glass windows and carving above the front door the motto "Do as thou will". The gardens boasted a statue of a naked Venus (bending over, so the unwary visitor walked into her buttocks) and a well-endowed statue of Priapus, who was the Greek fertility god of purely phallic character, protector of livestock, fruit plants, gardens and male genitalia.

Dashwood modeled the reconstruction after the temple at Palmyra, complete with Corinthian pillars. On the ceiling, he had a depiction of the Last Supper, the Christian version of the agape of the classical Mysteries, and a golden ball, seven feet in diameter, mounted on the church spire. This solar symbol was a copy of the golden ball on the Custom House in Venice, which has a weather vane constructed in the shape of the goddess Fortuna. This golden globe held seats inside for three people. It is believed this ball was meant to link the sun god who was born at the winter solstice with Christ as 'the Light of the World', a clear blurring of pagan and Christian ideals. At one end of the Abbey's dining room was a figure of Harpocrates, the Egyptian god of silence, with his finger to his lips, and an effigy of Angerona, the Roman goddess of silence. It has been said that these statues were reminders to the Friars that nothing that was said or went on in the Abbey was to be spoken about outside its walls. In Freemasonry, these two deities are known as "the guardians of secrecy". In 1740, the Earl of Middlesex had a medallion struck depicting Harpocrates when he became the Grand Master of the Masonic Lodge in Florence.

Dashwood's interest in pagan gods and goddesses were reflected in the decorations for his house at West Wycombe, designed by the famous architect, Robert Adam. The west wing of the building was a replica of a classical temple to Bacchus, complete with a statue of the god. On the ceiling, was a painting of Dionysus and Ariadne in chariots drawn by leopards and goats and followed by a company of satyrs and nymphs. Other representations of the two deities appear in the house and the myth would seem to have a special significance to Dashwood.

To celebrate the opening of the Bacchus temple, Dashwood organized a pageant with actors dressed as fauns, satyrs and nymphs in animal skins and ivy wreathes. The classical pagan theme continued in the garden, which, some writers claim, was laid out in the form of a naked woman. It certainly had many statues of classical gods and goddesses and small temples dedicated to Flora, Daphne, the four winds and music.

Around 1750, Dashwood arranged to have a network of caves built under West Wycombe Hill. The Friars for their meetings or, as local used these, and London gossip had it, their wild orgies. The entrance to the caves was surrounded by Yew trees and a low passageway led northwards to join several small caves and catacombs. These caves featured individual cells for the monks to entertain their female guests, and a banqueting hall. An underground stream, known to the monks at the River Styx, had to be crossed to give access to the Inner Sanctum, a circular room where so-called Black Masses were said to be performed.

Gerald Gardner claimed the caves represented the Goddess and stated "the banqueting hall represents the womb where new life originates. After being born in the womb, the worshippers pass through the pubic triangle and into the flowing river. Then born and purified they go on to the joys or resurrection that awaits them in the temple."

The members of the Hellfire Club included some of the most wealthy and influential people in the land. Thomas Potter (the son of the Archbishop of Canterbury and Paymaster General), the Lord Mayor of London, John Wilkes, the satirical artist, William Hogarth the Earl of Bute (who was Prime Minister), the Prince of Wales, possibly even Benjamin Franklin and the famous gothic author, Horace Walpole were suspected members . It was a place of luxury and debauchery that would have done Lord Byron proud, with the "monks" and prostitutes brought down the Thames from London in barges to act as masked "nuns". They celebrated the Black Mass over the naked bodies of aristocratic women. No doubt, this was the fact from history that kindled the fuel of the early days of Anton La Vey's Satanic rituals for his own Black Mass. It seems to have been an open secret among the members of the Establishment which Dashwood and his friends belonged to. When Dashwood became Chancellor, one of his first actions was to tax cider. This led to the circulation of a rhyme, saying "Dashwood shall pour from a communion cup / libations to the goddess without eyes / and hot or not in cider and excise", a pointed reference to the goddess Angerona.

A painting was also done of Dashwood depicting him dressed in a monk's habit and kneeling to worship a statue of Venus. One of the leading members, John Wilkes, gave the game away when he said "No profane eye has dared to penetrate the English Eleusinian Mysteries of the Chapter Room (the inner sanctum) where the monks assembled on solemn occasions" which in fact was the secret rites performed and libations to the Bona Dea. The latter was, of course, the title of the Great Mother Goddess in the classical Mysteries.

In his younger Days, Sir Francis Dashwood was a member of the Mount Haemus grove of druids, a group that claimed descent from a 13th century druidic grove established in Oxford. In turn, this grove claimed connections with the Mysteries of Ceridwen still practiced at that time in the Snowdonia region of

North Wales. The druidic Council of Eleven withdrew Dashwood's charter to run a grove, following rumors about sex orgies, a similar charge put to groups such as those lead by Crowley and Gardner later in merry old England.

The Hellfire Caves existed before Dashwood enlarged them. They were, in fact, prehistoric in origin and it is said that in ancient times a pagan altar used to exist on West Wycombe Hill with pagan catacombs below. The Friars were, therefore, using a long-established pagan site for their meetings.

As local legend says, a secret passageway leads from the caves to St. Lawrence's church. A mysterious Lady Mary or Sister Agnes, an abbess who was supposed to rule over the "nuns", apparently used for the tunnel for romantic trysts with her boyfriend who was the priest at the church! When asked about Sister Agnes, Dashwood would take his visitors to a hole in the wall of one of the passageways. When they looked through, they saw a "witch's face", illuminated by candles. In fact, this face was a mask.

As it were, in 1751, Dashwood paid for the church to be restored - an odd act for a so-called Satanist. However, one later visitor described his renovations as "an Egyptian hall" and said that the restored church "gives one not the last idea of a place sacred to religious worship". Primarily though, the monks attracted to the Order were merely "happy disciples of Bacchus and Venus who got together occasionally to celebrate women and wine". One 19th century commentator once said, "Sir Francis himself officiated as high priest...engaged in pouring a libation from a communion cup to the mysterious object of their homage" – a mysterious object of their homage was the Goddess. Although they may indeed have inspired LaVey's Satanist rituals, Sir Francis Dashwood and his merry monks were not "Devil worshipping Satanists." Rather they were hedonistic Masons following the ancient pagan Mysteries.

Pagan Masonic Architecture

During the bombing of England by the Nazis, the top of a church altar became dislodged, exposing an ancient stone phallus inside. Often the Church hid relics of their predecessors' faiths. This repulsion of old pagan ways, however, did not prevent Masons who built churches from including the Green Man in carvings, or the use of gargoyles and grotesques in Gothic cathedrals to ward off evil spirits. Paganism lay in the hearts of the early Masonic builders. Some fertility goddesses of the Celtic times were hidden among the carvings and some went so far as to depict homosexuality and bestiality of the monks! Perhaps this in some small way was vengeance for the Templars dying due to false accusations of the same thing. We will never know. What is clear to most students of the Masons is that the early brotherhood held fast to the political views of democracy and equality. This thinking eventually leads them to rebel against the tyranny connected to both the monarchy and The Church during the French and American Revolutions. The public image of associations using their influence in business trading and government stems from this, which is the reason my grand father and his father before him were

Masons and involved in both Law and Government. From the doctrines of King Solomon and his temple, Masons deem it their spiritual duty to perfect the temple of the body, symbolically as part of the Divine. The idea of divinity within all things carried over to the individual, so perfection and discipline was a hallmark of the members and remains so today.

Chapter Four

The Illuminati

Out of all the secret groups of the past, the Illuminati most likely have the largest amount of misinformation spread about them, especially the true intent of the group. Wild accusations of world government take over and control of the global populace has influence fiction more than the masses of people itself. Truth be told, the real intentions of this mysterious cabal was not very different from the Rosicrucians or Free Masons. The title Illuminati was applied to the French Martinists, a group which had been founded in 1754 by Martinez Pasqualis, and to their imitators the Russian Martinists, headed about 1790 by Professor Schwartz of Moscow. Both were occultist cabalists, absorbing eclectic ideas. This movement of freethinkers that were the most radical offshoot of The Enlightenment — whose adherents were given the name Illuminati (but who called themselves "Perfectibilists") — was founded on May 1, 1776 by Jesuit-taught Adam Weishaupt. Since Illuminati translates to "enlightened ones" in Latin, it is natural that several unrelated historical groups have identified themselves as Illuminati. Often, this was due to claims of possessing Gnostic texts or other arcane information not generally available.

87

Promethean Flame by Corvis Nocturnum
Adam Weishaupt

Adam Weishaupt was the best-known head of the society. The group has also been called the Illuminati Order, the Order of the Illuminati, the Ancient Illuminated Seers of Bavaria, and the Bavarian Illuminati. In 1777, Karl Theodor, Elector of Palatinate, succeeded as ruler of Bavaria. He was a proponent of Enlightened Despotism and in 1784; his government banned all secret societies, including the Illuminati and the Freemasons.

The structure of the Illuminati soon collapsed, but while it was in existence, many influential intellectuals and progressive politicians counted themselves as members. Its members were supposedly drawn primarily from Masons and former Masons, and although some Masons were known to be members, there is no evidence that Freemasons supported it. The members pledged obedience to their superiors, and were divided into three main classes: the first, known as the Nursery, encompassed the ascending degrees or offices of Preparation, Novice, Minerval and Illuminatus Minor; the second, known as the Masonry, consisting of the ascending degrees of Illuminatus Major and Illuminatus Dirigens, the latter also sometimes called Scotch Knight; the third, designated the Mysteries, was subdivided into the degrees of the

Lesser Mysteries (Presbyter and Regent) and those of the Greater Mysteries (Magus and Rex). Relations with Masonic Lodges were established at Munich in 1780.

The order had its branches in most countries of the European continent; its members were reportedly around 3,000 to 4,000 members in the span of 10 years. The scheme had its attraction for literary men, such as Goethe and Baudelaire. We will learn more on Goethe in the second part of this book.

The Illuminati is the name of many groups, modern and historical, real and fictitious, verified and alleged. Most commonly, however, The Illuminati refers specifically to the Bavarian Illuminati, perhaps the least secret of all secret societies in the world. Most use refers to an alleged shadowy conspiratorial organization that controls world affairs behind the scenes, usually a modern incarnation or continuation of the Bavarian Illuminati. Illuminati are sometimes used synonymously with New World Order. We see this struggle for power in the video game turned action films *Laura Croft Tomb Raider,* and *Laura Croft Cradle of Life*.

The movement, under the name of Illuminés, reached France from Seville in 1623, and attained a following in 1635. A century later, another, more obscure, body of Illuminés became known in the south of France in 1722, and appears to have lingered until 1794.

The Bavarian Illuminati have cast a long shadow in popular history thanks to the writings of their opponents. The lurid allegations of conspiracy that have colored the image of the Freemasons have almost overshadowed that of the Illuminati. Many claimed to present evidence of an Illuminati conspiracy striving to replace all religions with humanism and all nations with a single world government.

More recently, Anthony C. Sutton suggested that the secret society Skull and Bones was founded as the American branch of the Illuminati. Others think very similar groups like Scroll and Key had Illuminati origins as well. Thomas Jefferson claimed they intended to spread information and the principles of true morality. He attributed the secrecy of the Illuminati to what he called "the tyranny of a despot and priests". Templar Revelation by Lynn Picknett and Clive Prince speaks of how the beginnings of science were a threat to the might of the Vatican. One must realize, unlike today, that the Church not only dictated what people were to believe, but they governed monarchies as well. Copernicus' theory in 1630 challenging the Earth being the center of the Universe by saying the sun is what all planets revolved around created paranoia that Pagan sun worship would explode everywhere and such blasphemous ideas would destroy the ironclad grip of Church. Scientists used the four elements as extensively as did paganism, for different purposes; yet to the Vatican it held equal fear for the same reason. Sadly, during the enlightened period of the Renaissance many artists and scientists died for their heretical thoughts. Rationality challenged dogma, and the search for truth caused people to question. An even larger rift formed and the members of societies went further underground. One might argue that these groups as well as the Church sought (or still do) global domination, so that the few elite would rule over the commoner, whom would forever be ignorant of the truth. Every esoteric, religious, or government group tends to breed mistrust when they hold power, especially when members of any organization are behind closed doors wielding great the ability to influence others lives.

All seem to agree that the enemies of the Illuminati were the monarchs of Europe and the Church; and some claimed that the French revolution was engineered and controlled by the Illuminati and later theorists have claimed their responsibility for the Russian Revolution of 1917, although the order was officially shut down in 1790, we find more from the Illuminati. Often the symbol of the all-seeing pyramid in the Great Seal of the United States is used as an example of the Illuminati's ever-present watchful eye over Americans.

About the time that the Illuminati were outlawed in Bavaria, the Roman Catholic Church prohibited its members from joining Masonic lodges, on pain of excommunication. This was done as a general edict, since the Church believed many lodges to have been infiltrated and subverted by the Illuminati, but was not able to accurately ascertain which ones. This rule was relaxed only in the late 20th century.

Promethean Flame by Corvis Nocturnum
Francis Bacon

Bacon was an English philosopher, political leader and essayist. Rumor has it he was the illegitimate son of Queen Elizabeth I and the Earl of Leicester; however, I have found little written on whether that is fact or not. Bacon began his professional life as a lawyer, but was involved in a the goddess Athena-worshipping group called Order of Helmet, for Athena was goddess of both war and wisdom - he has become best known as a philosophical advocate and defender of the scientific revolution. He longed for a Utopian society were humanity lived in perfection. His works establish and popularize an inductive methodology for scientific inquiry, often called the Baconian method. Induction implies drawing knowledge from the natural world through experimentation, observation, and testing of hypotheses, now known as the scientific method. In the context of his time, such methods were connected with the occult trends of hermeticism and alchemy. I ran across an interesting fact about Bacon while doing my research. He used the story of the Sphinx, a creature of Egyptian myth, to relate his thoughts on science. In the tale, a man asks a question of the great beast who demands an answer to a riddle. What walks on four legs, then two, then three, and finally, on all four again? The answer was man – he crawls on all fours, stands upright, and then needs a walking stick in old age, then feeble, requires a bed with four legs until death. Bacon reasoned that in the pursuit of science (a dangerous thing in his day) that it be approached like the fearsome Sphinx, with care and reason, a lesson to all future generations of would be scientists.

Bacon entered Trinity College, Cambridge, in 1573 at the age of 12, living for three years there with his older brother Anthony Bacon. At Cambridge Bacon first met the Queen, who was impressed by his precocious intellect, and started calling him "the young Lord Keeper."

On June 27, 1576, Bacon entered De Societate Magistrorum at Gray's Inn, and a few months later went abroad with Sir Amias Paulet, the English ambassador at Paris. The disturbed state of government and society in France under Henry III afforded him valuable political instruction. The sudden death of his father in February 1579 necessitated Bacon's return to England, and seriously influenced his fortunes. Sir Nicholas had laid up a considerable sum of money to purchase an estate for his youngest son. Having started with insufficient means, he borrowed money and became habitually in debt. To support himself, Francis took up his residence in law at Gray's Inn in 1579.

In 1580, he applied for a post at court that might enable him to devote himself to a life of learning. His application failed, and for the next two years, he worked quietly at Gray's Inn giving himself seriously to the study of law. In 1584, he took a seat in parliament. In Parliament, he played a prominent part in urging the execution of Mary Queen of Scots. During this period Bacon became acquainted with Robert Devereux, 2nd Earl of Essex (1567-1601), Queen Elizabeth's favorite, as can be seen in the

1998 film *Elizabeth*, starring Cate Blanchett. During the next few years, his financial situation remained bleak. His friends could find no public office for him, a scheme for retrieving his position by a marriage with the wealthy widow Lady Elizabeth Hatton failed, and in 1598, he was arrested for debt. His standing in the Queen's eyes, however, was beginning to improve. He gradually acquired the standing of one of the learned counsel, though he had no commission or warrant and received no salary. His relationship with the Queen also improved when he severed ties with Essex, a fortunate move considering that the latter would be executed for treason in 1601. Bacon was one of those appointed to investigate the charges against him, and examine witnesses, in connection with which he showed an ungrateful and indecent eagerness in pressing the case against his former friend and benefactor.

The accession of James I did bring Bacon into greater favor. He was knighted in 1603, and endeavored to set himself right with the new powers by writing his *Apologie* of his proceedings in the case of Essex, who had favored the succession of James. In the course of the uneventful first parliament session, Bacon married Alice Barnham, the daughter of a well-connected London council member. Little is known of their married life save the fact that in his last will he disinherited her.

The supposed cause of Bacon's death is tragically ironic. In March of 1626, he came to London, and shortly after he became inspired by the possibility of using snow to preserve meat. Bacon purchased a chicken to investigate this possibility, but, during the endeavor of stuffing it with snow, contracted a fatal case of pneumonia. He died at Highgate on April 9 of 1626.

Works and philosophy

Bacon's works include his Essays, as well as *the Colours of Good and Evil* published in 1597. His famous aphorism, "knowledge is power", is found in the *Meditations*. Bacon also wrote in *Felicem Memoriam Elizabethae*, a eulogy for the Queen written in 1609, and various philosophical works that constitute the fragmentary and incomplete *Instauratio Magna*, the most important part of which is the *Novum Organum* (published 1620). He wrote the *Astrologia Sana* and expressed his belief that stars had physical effects on the planet. Although he did not propose an actual philosophy, but rather a method of developing philosophy; he wrote that, "whilst philosophy at the time used the deductive syllogism to interpret nature, the philosopher should instead proceed through inductive reasoning from fact to axiom to law."

Bacon's magnum opus was a novel called *The New Atlantis*, a tale of a family who had flying machines and implied that America was the New Atlantis. Bacon's developments of the inductive philosophy would revolutionize the future thought of the human race. He distinguishes between duty to the community, an ethical matter, and duty to God, a purely religious matter. He believed any moral action is the action of the human will, which is governed by reason and spurred on by the passions; habit is what aids men in directing their will toward the good and no universal rules can be made, as both situations and men's characters differ.

Bacon distinctly separated religion and philosophy, though the two can coexist. He stated, "Philosophy is based on reason, faith is based on revelation, and therefore irrational" and "the more discordant, therefore, and incredible, the divine mystery is, the more honor is shown to God in believing it, and the nobler is the victory of faith."

Chapter Five

The Golden Dawn

The beginning of a new age

The dawn of a new age of magic as claimed by most modern day new agers usually will by pass those before them and simply trace its theories and origins to Raymond Buckland, Gardner and Wicca, and Crowley, without giving pause to think of exactly were they derived their thoughts from. Nearly everyone on the path to wisdom of the ancients is familiar with a Tarot deck, regardless if they can use them or not, but very few know about the people who started them, or the origins of their development, nor how the items came into such wide use. The Order of the Golden Dawn started as a small group that became renowned during and shortly after the First and Second World War. Historically the group began as an extension of the Mysteries of Light, using Quabalah, Tarot, Astrology, Alchemy and Geomancy[3].

---

[3] Geomancy - A method of divination that interprets markings on the ground by tossing dirt.

Promethean Flame by Corvis Nocturnum
Order of the Golden Dawn

Hermetic Order of the Golden Dawn was the occult-oriented fraternal organization established by the Freemasons in England around 1888. Fred Hockley derived the order's rituals from writings, and members had to demonstrate competence in mysticism. The group influenced authors William B. Yeats and Algernon Blackwood.

Arthur Edward Waite

Arthur Edward Waite joined the Hermetic Order of the Golden Dawn in 1891 and entered the Societas Rosicruciana in Anglia in 1902. When he became Grand Master of the Order in 1903, he changed its name to the Holy Order the Golden Dawn. He was occultist who introduced a Rosicrucian influence to modern magic, and was the originator of the Rider-Waite deck of tarot cards. The 17th century Rosicrucians definitely had a considerable influence on Anglo-Saxon Masonry. The film *Ninth Gate*, starring Johnny Depp used authentic looking drawings from the same time period. Where as Waite influenced Neo- Pagans such as Gerald Gardner, the 1950's "father of Wicca"

his polar opposite Aleister Crowley. Crowley came to influence what is known as "the left hand path," or beliefs that centered on the energies of the universe focus *to* the individual is more important rather that to the benefit of the majority by using the energy of the universe to heal itself and others.

Most influential to the formation of the group was Samuel Liddell Macgregor Mathers, in Egyptian costume, performs a ritual of Isis (*not* a Rite of the Golden Dawn). The original Hermetic Order of the Golden Dawn, which was founded originally as "the Fraternity of the Hermetic Order of the Golden Dawn," a magical fraternity founded in London by Dr. William Wynn Mathers later evolved, continuing under at least two spin-off organizations, the Stella Matutina (Morning Star) and the Alpha et Omega. The Stella Matutina closed its doors in the United Kingdom before WWII, but continued to function in New Zealand until the late 1970s.

Influences on Golden Dawn concepts and work include freemasonry, theosophy, Eliphas Levi, Papus, Enochian Magic, and medieval grimoires. It has long been thought that the systemization of these influences into a new school of thought is largely the merit of Mathers, who at times was teaching things he had discovered only days or hours before. Mathers was responsible for the Rosicrucian inner order of the Golden Dawn being established where practical magic was taught.

The group was probably the single greatest influence on 20th century western occultism. While it existed, it was the focal point of the development and redevelopment of magical thinking in Europe. In it, most concepts of magic and ritual that have since become core elements of Wicca, Thelema, western mystery schools and other forms of magical spirituality were first formulated.

The Golden Dawn tradition is a branch of ceremonial magic most concerned with the concepts and practices developed by the Hermetic Order of the Golden Dawn. As of 2005, many more people consider themselves part of the Golden Dawn tradition than ever were members of the order led by Mathers.

In logical continuation of the Golden Dawn concept, many adherents of this tradition organize themselves into orders. These orders use organizational structures and teachings more or less closely related to those of the original order. It continued to spawn other groups, such as the Hermetic Order of the Golden Dawn, Inc., Ordo Stella Matutina, The Open Source Order of the Golden Dawn, Thelemic Order of the Golden Dawn, Esoteric Order of the Golden Dawn (formerly known as Hermetic Order of the Morning Star,) International, and Temple Auriel Hermetic Order of the Golden Dawn. Of all the members of the Golden Dawn, none was more famous than Aleister Crowley was.

Aleister Crowley

Aleister Crowley, born Edward Alexander Crowley (12 October 1875 – 1 December 1947) was an occultist, prolific writer, mystic, hedonist, and sexual revolutionary. His other interests and accomplishments were wide-ranging. He was a chess master, mountain climber, poet, painter, astrologer, drug experimenter, and social critic. Although highly regarded as beneficial as a magician, and I personally won't deny his influence on today's ideas, they were hardly unique. Crowley was not able to control his voracious appetites for drugs or sex. Self-control for a magician (his will be done) was clearly lacking. He is perhaps best known today for his occult writings, especially The Book of the Law, the central sacred text of his philosophical and religious system of Thelema. Crowley was also an influential member in several occult organizations, including the Golden Dawn, and Ordo Templi Orientis. He gained much notoriety during his lifetime, and was famously dubbed "The Wickedest Man In the World."

Aleister grew up in a staunch Plymouth Brethren household. His father, after retiring from his Daily duties as a brewer, took up the practice of preaching at a fanatical pace. Daily Bible studies and private tutoring were mainstays in young Aleister's childhood. However, after his father's death, his mother's efforts at indoctrinating her son in the Christian faith only served to provoke Aleister's skepticism. As a child, young Aleister's constant rebellious behavior displeased his devout mother to such an extent she would chastise him by calling him "The Beast" (from the Book of Revelation), an epithet that Crowley would later happily adopt for himself. He objected to the labeling of what he saw as life's most worthwhile and enjoyable activities as "sinful".

In response, Crowley created his own philosophical system, Scientific Illuminism — a synthesis of various Eastern mystical systems (including Hinduism, Buddhism, Tantra, the predecessor to Western sex Magick, Zoroastrianism and the many systems of Yoga) fused with the Western occult sciences of the Hermetic Order of the Golden Dawn. In addition, the many reformed rituals of Freemasonry he later reformulated within the Ordo Templi Orientis (O.T.O.). Crowley coined the term "Magick" to describe this system, which also appeals to scientific and philosophical skepticism. His undergraduate studies in chemistry at Trinity College, Cambridge helped forge the scientific skepticism that later culminated in the many-volumes and unparalleled occult publication, *The Equinox.*

Following the death of his father, the young Aleister (then "Alec" or "Alick") turned to a form of Satanism in grief. In other words, he decided to rebel against the God of his upbringing. However, within a few years he abandoned this for atheism and hedonism, or in his words, "began to behave like a normal, healthy human being." During the year 1897, he slowly came to view earthly pursuits as useless and began his lifelong exploration of esoteric matters. A number of events contributed to this change.

Involved as a young adult in the Hermetic Order of the Golden Dawn, he first studied mysticism with and made enemies of William Butler Yeats and Arthur Edward Waite. Like many in occult circles of the time, Crowley voiced the view that Waite was a pretentious bore through critiques of Waite's writings and editorials of many of his contemporary authors' writings.

His friend and Golden Dawn associate Allan Bennett introduced him to the ideas of Buddhism. Several decades after Crowley's participation in the Golden Dawn, Mathers claimed copyright protection over a particular ritual and sued Crowley for infringement after Crowley's public display of the ritual. While the public trial continued, both Mathers and Crowley claimed to call forth armies of demons and angels to fight on behalf of their summoner. Both also developed and carried complex Seal of Solomon amulets and talismans. A similar piece can be found in Azure Green catalogues, one of the largest magic shops online.

In a book of fiction entitled *Moonchild*, Crowley portrayed Mathers as the primary villain, including him as a character named SRMD, using the abbreviation of Mathers' magical name. Arthur Edward Waite also appeared in *Moonchild* as a villain named Arthwaite, while Bennett appeared in *Moonchild* as the main character's wise mentor, Simon Iff. While he did not officially break with Mathers until 1904, Crowley lost faith in this teacher's abilities soon after the 1900 schism. Later that year, Crowley traveled to Mexico and continued his magical studies in isolation. His writings suggest that he discovered the word Abraha Dabra during this time. In October of 1901, after practicing Raja Yoga for some time, he said he had reached a state he called dhyana — one of many states of unification in thoughts that are described in *Magick Book IV*, in which he gave meditation as the means of attaining his goal. The essay describes ceremonial Magick as a means of training the will, and of constantly directing one's thoughts to a given object through ritual. A year later in his 1903 essay, *Science and Buddhism*, Crowley urged an empirical approach to Buddhist teachings.

He said that a mystical experience in 1904 while on vacation in Cairo, Egypt, led to his founding of the religious philosophy known as Thelema. Aleister's wife Rose started to behave in an odd way, and this led him to think that some entity had made contact with her. At her instructions, he performed an invocation of the Egyptian god Horus on March 20 with "great success". According to Crowley, the god told him that a new magical Aeon was begun, with Crowley serving as its prophet. Rose continued to tell Crowley in detail to await a further revelation. On April 8, and for the following two Days, at exactly noon he heard a voice, dictating the words of the text, *The Book of the Law*. The voice claimed to be that of Horus, the god of force and fire, child of Isis and Osiris and self-appointed conquering lord of the New Aeon, via his chosen scribe "the prince-priest the

Beast." Hallucinations or excessive drug use, we will never be sure what exactly prompted his bizarre writings.

Portions of the book are in numerical cipher, which Crowley claimed the inability to decipher – that would seem to strike me as oddly telling. Thelemic explains this by pointing to a warning within the *Book of the Law* — the speaker supposedly warned that the scribe, Aleister Crowley, was never to attempt to decode the ciphers, for to do so would end only in folly. To me, this was a clear case of hoodwinking an extremely gullible audience! While he declared a "new Equinox of the Gods" in early 1904, supposedly passing on the revelation of March 20 to the occult community, it took years for Crowley to fully accept the writing of the *Book of the Law* and follow its doctrine. Only after countless attempts to test its writings did he come to embrace them as the official doctrine of the *New Aeon of Horus*.

In 1934 Crowley was declared bankrupt after losing a court case in which he sued the artist Nina Hamnett for calling him a black magician in her 1932 book, *Laughing Torso*. In addressing the jury, Mr. Justice Swift said, "I have been over forty years engaged in the administration of the law in one capacity or another. I thought that I knew of every conceivable form of wickedness. I thought that everything which was vicious and bad had been produced at one time or another before me. I have learnt in this case that we can always learn something more if we live long enough. I have never heard such dreadful, horrible, blasphemous and abominable stuff as that which has been produced by the man

(Crowley) who describes himself to you as the greatest living poet."

Aleister Crowley died of a respiratory infection in a Hastings boarding house in December 1947, at the age of 72. He was penniless and addicted to opium, which had supposedly been prescribed for his asthma and bronchitis, at the time.

O.T.O. and Aleister Crowley

Another fairly large influence on the Golden Dawn was Theodore Reuss, who met Aleister Crowley and in 1910 admitted him to the three degrees of O.T.O. Just two years later Crowley was placed in charge of both Great Britain and Ireland branches of the Order. The appointment included the operation of the Masonic degrees of O.T.O., which were called Mysteria Mystica Maxima. Within the year, Crowley had written the Manifesto, which described the basic ten-degree system, which was still principally Masonic. Around 1914, soon after the First World War began, he moved to America. It was around this time that he decided to integrate Thelema into the O.T.O. system. The founding of Ordo Templi Orientis began with a wealthy paper chemist, Carl Kellner (1851-1905). A student of the occult and familiar with several modern secret organizations, he had come to believe that he had discovered a "Key" to the symbolism of Freemasonry and to the Mysteries of Nature itself. He then aspired to create an Academia Masonica that would unify the various systems of Masonry. Kellner, along with associate, Theodor Reuss (1855-1923), decided to call it the Oriental Templar Order. In 1902, Reuss, along with

Franz Hartmann and Henry Klein, purchased the right to perform the Scottish, Memphis and Mizraim rites of Freemasonry, the authority of which confirmed in 1904 and again in 1905. These rites formed the core of the newly established Order. When Kellner died in 1905, Reuss assumed full control, becoming the first Outer Head of the Order.

Crowley wrote that Theodor Reuss suffered a stroke in 1920 and expressed doubts about Reuss's competence to retain his office. Understandably, this caused relations between Reuss and Crowley to deteriorate. Crowley informed Reuss that he was proclaiming himself the Outer Head of the Order. Reuss died on October 28, 1923 leaving Crowley free to claim in later correspondence that Reuss had designated him as his successor. However, no other candiDate at the time bothered to step forward to refute Crowley by offering proof of succession.

The Ordo Templi Orientis

The Ordo Templi Orientis (O.T.O.), Order of the Temple of the East, or the Order of Oriental Templars is an international fraternal and religious organization. For its teachings and principles of organization, it was the first organization to accept the Law of Thelema, which is expressed as "Do what thou wilt shall be the whole of the Law." Thelemites believe that this Law became firmly established with the writing of the *Book of Law*.

The Book of the Law is the central sacred text of Thelema, written (or received) by Aleister Crowley in Cairo, Egypt in the year 1904. It contains three chapters, each of which was written down in one hour, beginning at noon, on April 8th, 9th, and 10th. Crowley claims that the author was an entity named Aiwass, whom he later identified as his own Holy Guardian Angel (or "Secret Self"). The teachings within this small book are expressed as the Law of Thelema, usually encapsulated by these two phrases:

"Do what thou wilt shall be the whole of the Law", and "Love is the law, love under will". The religious or mystical system that Crowley founded, into which most of his writings fall, he named Thelema. Thelema combines a radical form of philosophical libertarianism, akin in some ways to Nietzsche, with a mystical initiatory system derived in part from the Golden Dawn. Chief among the precepts of Thelema is the sovereignty of the individual will: "Do what thou wilt shall be the whole of the Law." Crowley's idea of will, however, is not simply the individual's desires or wishes, but also incorporates a sense of the person's destiny or greater purpose: what he termed "True Will." Much of the initiatory system of Thelema is focused on discovering and manifesting one's Will, culminating in what he termed Knowledge and Conversation with the Holy Guardian Angel (See: Thelemic mysticism). Much else is devoted to an Eastern-inspired dissolution of the individual ego, as a means to that end.

The second precept of Thelema is "Love is the law, love under will," Crowley's meaning of "Love" is as complex as that of "Will". It is frequently sexual. Crowley's system, like elements of the Golden Dawn before him, sees the dichotomy and tension between the male and female as funDamental to existence, and sexual "Magick" and metaphor form a significant part of Thelemic ritual. However, Love is also discussed as the Union of Opposites, which Crowley thought was the key to enlightenment.

Thelema draws on numerous older sources and, like many other new religious movements of its time, combines "Western" and "Eastern" traditions.

Crowley claimed to use a scientific method to study what people at the time called "spiritual" experiences, making "The Method of Science, the Aim of Religion" the catchphrase of his magazine *The Equinox*. By this, he meant that mystical experiences should not be taken at face value, but critiqued and experimented with in order to arrive at their underlying religious meaning. In this he may be considered to foreshadow Dr. Timothy Leary, who at one point sought to apply the same method to psychedelic drug experiences. Yet like Leary's, Crowley's method has received little "scientific" attention outside the circle of Thelema's practitioners.

Crowley's magical and initiatory system has amongst its innermost reaches a set of teachings on sex "Magick." He frequently expressed views about sex that were radical for his time, and published numerous poems and tracts combining pagan religious themes with sexual imagery both heterosexual and homosexual. Sex Magick is the use of the sex act—or the energies, passions or arousal states it evokes—as a point upon which to focus the will or magical desire for effects in the non-sexual world. In this, Crowley was inspired by Paschal Beverly Randolph, an

American author writing in the 1870s who wrote (in his book *Eulis*) of using the "nuptive moment" (orgasm) as the time to make a "prayer" for events to occur.

Within the subject of occultism Crowley wrote widely, penning commentaries on Magick, the Tarot, Yoga, the Quabalah, astrology, and numerous other subjects. He also wrote a Thelemic "translation" of the Tao Te Ching, based on earlier English translations since he knew little or no Chinese. Like the Golden Dawn mystics before him, Crowley evidently sought to comprehend the entire human religious and mystical experience in a single philosophy.

Crowley in popular culture

Crowley has exerted an enduring influence in popular culture, including tributes from rock musicians such as Jimmy Page, Ozzy Osbourne, Cradle of Filth and The Beatles (his face appeared on their album, Sergeant Pepper's Lonely Hearts Club Band. Crowley remains a popular icon of libertines and those interested in the theory of Magick.

Very similar in its structure to that of Freemasonry, with a series of graded initiations. The O.T.O. also includes the Ecclesia Gnostic Catholica or Gnostic Catholic Church, which is the ecclesiastical arm of the Order. Its central rite, which is public, is called Liber XV, or the Gnostic Mass. O.T.O. claims over 3000 members in 58 countries; about half of these are in the United States.

The O.T.O. was described by Crowley as the "first of the great Old Æon orders to accept The Book of the Law". O.T.O. borrowed material from European and U.S. irregular Masonic organizations, and although some Masonic symbolism and language is in use, their context is no longer that of Freemasonry, but of Thelema and its tenets. "The Order offers esoteric instruction through dramatic ritual, guidance in a system of illuminated ethics, and fellowship among aspirants to the Great Work of realizing the divine in the human" O.T.O. has two core areas of ritual activity: initiation into the Mysteries, and the celebration of Liber XV, the Gnostic Mass. In addition, the Order organizes lectures, classes, social events, theatrical productions and artistic exhibitions; publishes books and journals; and provides instruction in Hermetic science, yoga, and Magick.

Crowley wrote in his Confessions, "The O.T.O. is in possession of one supreme secret. The whole of its system [is] directed towards communicating to its members, by progressively plain hints, this all-important instruction." Of the first set of initiations, "the main objects of the instruction [are] two. It [is] firstly necessary to explain the universe and the relations of human life therewith. Secondly, to instruct every man [and woman] how best to adapt his [or her] life to the cosmos and to develop his faculties to the utmost advantage. I accordingly constructed a series of rituals, Minerval, Man, Magician, Master-Magician, Perfect Magician and Perfect Initiate, which should illustrate the course of human life in its largest philosophical aspect." The initiation rituals after the V° are such that "the candidate is instructed in the value of discretion, loyalty, independence, truthfulness, courage, self-control, indifference to circumstance, impartiality, skepticism, and other virtues, and at the same time assisted him to discover for himself the nature of [the supreme] secret, the proper object of its employment and the best means for insuring success for its use."

Of the entire system of O.T.O., Crowley wrote in Confessions: It offers a rational basis for universal brotherhood and for universal religion. It puts forward a scientific statement which is a summary of all that is at present known about the universe by means of a simple, yet sublime symbolism, artistically arranged. It also enables each man to discover for himself his personal destiny, indicates the moral and intellectual qualities which he requires in order to fulfill it freely, and finally puts in his hands an unimaginably powerful weapon which he may use to develop in himself every faculty which he may need in his work. (Pg. 703)

There are thirteen numbered degrees and twelve un-numbered. They are divided into three grades or "triads": the Hermit, the Lover, and the Man of Earth. Admittance to each degree of O.T.O. involves an initiation and the swearing of an oath similar to those used in Freemasonry. The ultimate goal of initiation in O.T.O thereby to is "to instruct the individual by allegory and symbol in the profound mysteries of Nature, and assist each to discover his or her own true Identity."

Promethean Flame by Corvis Nocturnum

William Butler Yeats

Yeats, widely known as an Irish poet was also a mystic. Although born to a Protestant mother and father, was perhaps the primary driving force behind the Irish Literary Revival and was co-founder of the Abbey Theatre. Later on, Yeats also served as an Irish Senator. His early poetry drew heavily on Irish myth and folklore. His major influence in these years - and probably throughout the rest of his career as well - was Percy Bysshe Shelley, about whom we will read more in part two.

Yeats then was awarded the Nobel Prize for literature in 1923 for what the Nobel Committee described as "his always inspired poetry, which in a highly artistic form gives expression to the spirit of a whole nation."

He read extensively on the subjects of mysticism, spiritualism, occultism and astrology. Yeats was admitted into the *Golden Dawn* in March 1890, taking the name *Demon est Deus inversus*, translated as *Devil is the reverse of God*, this name being taken from the writings of Madame Blavatsky in which she discussed that "...even that divine Homogeneity must contain in itself the essence of both good and evil."

During his time as a senator, Yeats warned his colleagues "If you show that this country, southern Ireland, is going to be governed by Roman Catholic ideas and by Catholic ideas alone, you will never get the North ... You will put a wedge in the midst of this nation." As they were nearly all Catholics, they were of course offended by these comments.

Yeats wrote prolifically through the final years of his life, publishing poetry, plays and prose. His name even saw use in the futuristic film *Equilibrium*, starring Christian Bale. In this *Matrix* like futuristic post apocalypse masterpiece, fiction, poetry and feeling itself was attributed to the wars and hate of the human race. In order to prevent evil, the world government began burning books, art, and anything relating to the past. Drugs kept people zombie like, as they were not allowed to feel anything, and those refusing to conform were executed by fire – a futuristic Inquisition. Similarities arose in the movie again from our past, with burning of the libraries, as they did during the Dark Ages. One of the accused heretics, a former officer in it quoted, "Tread softly, for you're treading on my dreams" from a Yeats poem. Another quote of Yeats can be found in the beginning of the movie *The Anarchist Cookbook*.

After suffering from a variety of illnesses for a number of years, Yeats died at the Hôtel Idéal Séjour, in France in 1939 at age 73.

Dion Fortune

Dion Fortune was born in December of 1890 in North Wales. Her interest in the occult began while working as a psychotherapist just before the First World War. Her teacher was Theodore Moriarty, who specialized in Astro-psychological conditions. She joined the Golden Dawn in 1919.

A year later, she moved to London and began writing articles, which enraged Moina Mathers, who felt that Dion Fortune was betraying the secrets of the Order. Dion Fortune became increasingly disillusioned with the Golden Dawn, and after Dr. Moriarty's death in 1921 she set about founding her own esoteric order with a few of Moriarty's students.

After forming the Society of Inner Light, she and the others began working in trance medium; the techniques became vital to her studies and are still the basis for workings today. *The Mystical Kabbalah* and *The Cosmic Doctrine* are largely basics books and on mysticism and mediumship.

She took an interest in Crowley's work, especially his Thoth deck of Tarot styled cards. Crowley dedicated a book to her and both of the prominent magicians performed rituals during the Second World War against Germany.

Dion Fortune wrote about Psychic Vampires who drained ones vitality through misuse of other's resources, physical and mental, no doubt influencing writing by Anton LaVey in the 1960's in the *Satanic Bible*. Fortune died of leukemia in London at age 55.

Gerald Gardner

Gerald Gardner's family was no stranger to witchcraft. According to Gardner, one of his ancestors was burned as a witch in 1610, and even Gardner's own grandfather married a woman who was rumored to be a witch.

Due to his asthma, Gardner spent most of his childhood traveling through Europe with his nurse. This traveling awoke in him an interest in other cultures, other religions and other ways of life.

Later, he married and returned to England as a base home, but continued to travel abroad for archeological pursuits. Experiences that convinced him of a past life in Cyprus, led to his second book *A Goddess Arrives*, a fictional novel. Gardner's involvement in a local Masonic group, the Fellowship of Crotona, was were he became introduced to a coven of hereditary witches who claimed to be practicing rites handed down from the Middle Ages.

Witchcraft happened to be illegal in England, so Gardner was unable to write publicly about what he was learning. In 1949, he published another fictional novel called *High Magic's Aid*, under the name Scire. Much of the material in the story was actually based on the rituals of his coven. Later, when England repealed its witchcraft laws in the early 1950's, Gardner began his own coven. During this time, he coined the term skyclad, the practice of performing ritual in the nude. This is hardly an oddity coming from Gardner, who was a nudist long before being into witchcraft. My colleague Timothy Ringenberg agrees with my theory that Gardner's original goal creating in the formation of covens were for his ravenous sexual orgies. I allege Crowley was very similar, albeit with more sincerity in his occult pursuits!

Gardner's work began its way towards a more mainstream audience when Gardner wrote his first non-fiction book on witchcraft, *Witchcraft Today*. He gained notoriety as Britain's "Chief Witch". Though he did not enjoy the spotlight, he published a second book on the subject, *The Meaning of Witchcraft*.

In 1964, Gerald Gardner died at sea on a ship returning from Lebanon. Although much of his work truly revived the old witchcraft practices, and reshaped the world's view of alternative religion, not all practitioners today who are witches claim Wicca as their faith. As my dear friend Starr pointed out, Wicca is a denomination of Paganism, taking elements of pre-existing rituals styles and ideas. Witchcraft and Wicca are not the same thing. Not all Wiccans are Witches and not all Witches are Wiccans though it is possible to be both. Gardner was simply the first to label it under a new term. A fascinating book by Aidan Kelly *Crafting the Art of Magic* dissects Gardner's witch religion, showing rather convincingly that this was not a revival at all, but a redressing of Crowley and other similar era magicians occult works.

When newagers and online witches claim to be of generations of Wiccans, they seriously need study the era in which times Gardner truly lived!

Hitler and the Thule Society

Adolf Hitler joined a secret society called the Thule Society in 1919. It was in this group that he found the perverted beliefs that were later to lead him in his control of the German government - in the Thule Society: "... the sun played a prime role... as a sacred symbol of the Aryans, in contrast to... the moon, revered by the Semitic peoples. The Fuhrer saw in the Jewish people, with their black hair and swarthy complexions, the dark side of the human species, whilst the blond and blue-eyed Aryans constituted the light side of humanity. ... Hitler undertook to extirpate from the material world its impure elements." In addition to sun (or light) worship, the Thule Society also was incorrectly accused of the practice of Satan worship: "The inner core within the Thule Society were all Satanists who practiced Black Magic." We see the hint of the Thule in *Hellboy*, with Rasputin as the leader! In truth, however, the aim of the Society was a revival of Aryan Paganism.

The Thule Society was not a working-man's group as it included amongst its members: "judges, police-chiefs, barristers, lawyers, university professors and lecturers, aristocratic families, leading industrialists, surgeons, physicians, scientists, as well as a host of rich and influential bourgeois.... " The membership of the Thule Society also became the bedrock of the Nazi Party: "... the Committee and the forty original members of the New German Workers' Party were all drawn from the most powerful occult society in Germany—the Thule Society."

One of the founders of both groups, the Nazi Party and the Thule Society, was Dietrich Eckart: "a dedicated Satanist," not to be confused with modern day Satanists via Anton LaVey - which did not occur until the 1960's. Considered to be a supreme adept of the arts and rituals of Black Magic and the central figure in a powerful and wide-spread circle of occultists—the Thule Group. Eckart, one of the seven founder members of the Nazi Party, implemented the emblem of the Thule Society depicting a German dagger over a swastika of curved legs inscribed in a circle.

It is very possible that Hitler discovered his Jewish background and his relation to the Rothschild family, and with being aware of their enormous power to make or break European governments; he may have re-established contact with the family for a multitude of less than altruistic reasons. This would partially explain the enormous support he received from the international banking fraternity, which was closely entwined with the Rothschild family. Foremost, Hitler wanted to silence those who he believed knew that he was a descendant of the Rothschild's, and secondly, he wished to remove all traces of his ancestry from the Austrian records.

During his studies, Adolf Hitler commented on the Masons by saying, "All the supposed abominations, the skeletons and death's head, the coffins and the mysteries, are mere bogeys for children. But there is one dangerous element and that is the element I have copied from them. They form a sort of priestly nobility. They have developed and esoteric doctrine more merely formulated, but imparted through the symbols and mysteries in degrees of initiation. The hierarchical organization and the initiation through symbolic rites, that is to say, without bothering the brain by working on the imagination through magic and the symbols of a cult, all this has a dangerous element, and the element I have taken over. Don't you see that our party must be of this character...? An Order, the hierarchical Order of a secular priesthood."

However, Hitler despised the goodwill and Jewish basics of Quabalah of the early Masons and The Rosicrucians; despite the fact, his instructor Stebendorf was a freemason. The Swastika is a powerful magical symbol still used in High Masonic Degrees today. It is the Ancient "Futhark" Rune Script for the letter "G", the most important and universal symbol in Freemasonry. It was to replace the Cross-in the post Christian pagan religion of the Nazi's Occultism. Masonry symbols are represented in movies such as *League of Extraordinary Gentlemen*, where in the library, where the unlikely band of classic characters fighting a villain (thinly disguised as Hitler meets Moriarty of Sherlock Holmes fame) we see a Masonic emblem on the door.

The book *Christianity and American Freemasonry* by William J. Whalen (Our Sunday Visitor: 1987, pgs 23-25) discusses the racism of Freemasonry at some length; an organization dedicated to goodwill, Masonry ironically remains racially segregated in the United States. By 1987, decades after most American institutions had accepted racial integration; only four of the forty-nine Grand Lodges could count even one black member in their jurisdictions. As the author of a recent scholarly study of black Freemasonry observes, "The legitimation of social intermingling between black and white Masons has remained anathema in mainstream Freemasonry."' From the *Handbook of Secret Organizations* by Whalen. Perhaps this is part of Hitler's idea that the United States of America would condone his actions – he in fact used the actions of early US Army against the Native Americans, including chemical warfare (smallpox riddled blankets) and firing squads – the Gattling gun, designed for use in the Civil War, yet did not see use until the Calvary used it against the Lakota people of the late 1880's – was copied. During Hitler's stay in jail, he studied America and wrote *Mein Kampf*, outlining his plans.

Madame Helena Petrovna Blavatsky

A definite Thule contributor was a 33 degree Mason, Madame Helena Petrovna Blavatsky (1831-1891). She was born in what is now the Ukraine. She would be forty-four years old before creating the Society for which she is best remembered.

Blavatsky created a blend of Eastern religion and mysticism, European mythology and Egyptian occultism, and her style, as some authors have written, was evidence that science was going too far toward "proving" the errors of faith and that the average person embraced the quasi-scientific approach toward life. Nietzsche's God is Dead in *The Gay Science* in 1882 clearly pointed out man has ceased to be held back by a fear of an omnipotent being.

Darwin had published *The Origin of Species* in 1859 and the *Descent of Man* followed this in 1871. Both books offered evolution as the means by which humans were created, as opposed to the Biblical account found in Genesis. We'll learn more about Darwin's influence on philosophy in the second half of the book. The effect of the theory of evolution on religion was as great then as it is now. The controversy over Darwinism caused many people to question the existence of God, the possibility of redemption, life after death, etc. People were startled to discover that Biblical myths were at odds with scientific theories, and thus began to doubt everything they ever believed. They found themselves spiritually detached.

Blavatsky provided a much-appreciated antidote to Darwin, even as she was brazenly appropriating (and reversing) his theory of evolution. Her ideas were actually quite brilliant for her time, for they enabled intelligent and educated men and women to maintain deep spiritual beliefs while simultaneously acknowledging the inroads made by scientific research into areas previously considered beyond the domain of mere human knowledge. Blavatsky outlines evolution beyond Darwin to include vanished races up through the present imperfect race of humans, and continuing on into the future. The German occultists would later pick up the *Secret Doctrine's* message. The smug and condescending attitude of scientists and their devotees toward the "unscientific" and mystics began to satisfy the requirements of science in what are patently unscientific pursuits. Science still reeled from furor caused by Galileo and Copernicus clashing with the papacy, then along came Blavatsky, who took new scientific attitudes as they were largely accepted and spun them into a mystical fashion.

Taking her ideas from Darwin, she popularized the notion of a spiritual struggle between various "races", and of the inherent superiority of the "Aryan" race, hypothetically the latest in the line of spiritual evolution. Blavatsky would borrow heavily from carefully chosen scientific authors in fields like archaeology and astronomy to bolster her arguments for the existence of Atlantis, extraterrestrial life forms, the creation of animals by humans (as opposed to the Darwinian line of succession), and more. Her work, Stanzas of Dyzan from *The Secret Doctrine* has a creation-myth story, were she describes seven figures of clay, much like the Scandinavian Eddas, a concept of man created by the "Sons of God" and according to Blavatsky "descending on Earth, where, after culling seven Manragoras, animated these roots, which became forthwith men." It strikes me as similar to the *Book of Enoch*, which was cut from the Bible along with other segments hidden from Jewish scrolls, (including the famous Dead Sea Scrolls) which speak of the Watcher Angels. In traditional angelology, angels are beings that exist between spirit and flesh, neither male nor female, occupying a space beneath God but above mankind. The Watcher tradition, in contrast, describes heavenly beings who are nevertheless earthly enough to sire children. They came to Earth to mate with mortal women, producing giant children. After teaching magic to them, the children became mighty leaders. The Bible contains lingering traces of this excised story, referring to the Watchers' children as "giants" and "men of renown." The children of the Watcher angels, variously referred to as Giborrim, Anakim, and Nephilim, founded a great and warlike empire, and when God saw this, he destroyed them in the Great Flood. In the canonized versions of the Bible, only the story of the Flood remains, its real reasons obscured.

The idea that beings who were more than human walked out of heaven to populate material reality with forbidden divine gifts has a great appeal within many of the darker subcultures. Among the modern vampire community, the stories of the Watchers has taken a new life. The band Nox Arcana released a CD with author/singer Michelle Belanger that retells the myth of the Nephilim in an epic fashion. The CD, entitled *Blood of Angels,* contains references to vampires, spirits, and fallen angels, all weaving an overall story of forbidden passions and the courage required to take what one wants.

John Dee and his Angelic writings and codes have played a part in the fascination of the Watcher Angels, yet he more than likely did not read the actual *Book of Enoch*, as one of the only surviving copies of this text was not discovered until years later, at the end of the eighteenth century. Interestingly, one of the first Western writers to make much of this forbidden text was the

Romantic poet, Lord Byron. Not only did he strongly identify himself with the leader of the Watchers, Shemyaza, but he also wrote at least one play inspired by the epic story.

Blavatsky's works--notably *Isis Unveiled* and *The Secret Doctrine*--appear to be the result of prodigious scholarship and were very convincing in their time. The rationale behind many later Nazi projects can be traced back to ideas first popularized by Blavatsky. A caste system of races, the superiority of the an "initiated" version of astrology and astronomy, the cosmic truths coded within pagan myths ... all of these and more can be found in the ideology of its dark creature, the SS. After all, Blavatsky pointed out the supreme occult significance of the swastika. Moreover, it was a follower of Blavatsky who was instrumental in introducing the *Protocols of the Elders of Zion* to a Western European community highly eager for a scapegoat.

Anxious to be in Hitler's good graces, some Nazi leaders repudiated Christianity. They wanted to set up a pagan cult of "blood, race, and soil." They would go back to the dark ritual of dramatic rites of their ancestors, although Hitler wished to be thought of publicly as Christian. Hitler was even seen signing a treaty with the Pope. The actions, or rather lack of action, by the Church, were publicly apologized for much later. The New Pagans resurrected Odin, Thor, and the old gods of primitive Teutons before Christ' time. Instead of the Old Testament, they adopted Nordic sagas and fairy tales. They set up a new trinity for worship under the aspects of bravery, loyalty, and physical force.

About 1932 members of the Nazi Party were in danger of defecting to other political organizations. Hitler's own trusted disciples were dividing the Party into warring factions that could not be controlled. On Halloween night - the pagan Sabbat of Samhain - his mistress Eva Braun shot herself. Despite the fact that Eva survived what the doctors would later characterize as ' 'serious suicide attempt', Hitler himself knew he was politically dead. It appeared as if he had lost the will to fight, and he began to speak more and more of his own death.

Neopaganism

According to the religoustolerance.org website, the term "pagan" means: "originally from the Latin 'paganus', which appears to have originally had such meanings as 'villager', 'country dweller', or 'hick'. The Roman army used it to refer to civilians. The early Roman Christians used "pagan" to refer to everyone who preferred to worship pre-Christian divinities, whom the Christians had decided were all "really" demons in disguise. Rural folk held on to their old faiths longer than city folks, and were unwilling to enroll in "the Army of the Lord." As time passed over the centuries, "pagan" became simply an insult, applied to the monotheistic followers of Islam by the Christians (and vice versa), and by the Protestants and Catholics towards each other, as it gradually gained the connotation of "a false religion and its followers." Later on during the beginning of the twentieth century, the word's primary meanings became a blend of "atheist," "agnostic," "hedonist," when referring to an educated, white, male, heterosexual, non-Celtic European as well as an "ignorant savage and/or pervert."

Today there are many people who proudly call themselves "Pagan," and use the word differently from the ways than the average laymen, past or present would. To the majority of practitioners, "Paganism" is a general term for polytheistic religions old and new, with "Pagan" used as the adjective as well as the membership term.

"Paleopaganism" or "Paleo-Paganism" is a general term for the original polytheistic, nature-centered faiths of tribal Europe, Africa, Asia, the Americas, Oceania and Australia, when they were (or in some rare cases, still are) practiced as intact belief systems. The "Great Religions of the World," Hinduism (prior to the influx of Islam into India), Taoism and Shinto, for example, fall under this category, though many members of these faiths might be reluctant to use the term. Some Paleopagan belief systems may be racist, sexist, homophobic, etc. There are billions of Paleopagans living and worshiping their deities today.

"Mesopaganism" or "Meso-Paganism" is a general term for a variety of movements, organized or not, started as attempts to recreate, or continue what their founders thought were the best aspects of the Paleopagan ways of their ancestors or predecessors. This in turn was heavily influenced accidentally, deliberately or involuntarily by concepts and practices from the religions such as Judaism, Christianity, Islam, or early Buddhism. Examples of Mesopagan belief systems would include Freemasonry,

Rosicrucianism, Spiritualism, as well as those forms of Druidism influenced by those movements, several sects of Hinduism that have been influenced by Islam and Christianity, Mahayana Buddhism, Aleister Crowley's religion/philosophy of Thelema, Odinism, most "Family Traditions" of Witchcraft and "British Traditionalist" denominations of Wicca.

Also included would be the so-called "Christo-Pagans," those who call themselves "monotheist Pagans," or mix Christianity with Pagan elements. Paganism - or more correctly, Neo-Paganism, like Gardner's Wicca, is a revival of ancient (mostly European) pre-Christian religions. There is a strong emphasis on fertility religions and the female/Goddess principle, as seen in *The Wicker Man*, especially the 2006 remake. The approach overall is very nondogmatic, with everyone free to adopt their own interpretation - the exact opposite to fundamentalist esoteric monotheism. There is also a strong emphasis on "Magick" and occultism, which is a strong link between Neo-Paganism and contemporary Hermeticism in general.

The most prominent of the Neo-Pagan religions is Wicca (meaning "Wise ones"), claiming to Date back to the Old Stone Age but in it fact was founded in the 1940s by Gerald Gardner, and itself split into a number of sects. The original Wicca of Gardner and Alex Sanders (Gardnerian and Alexandrian Wicca), although still quite big in England, has been largely supplanted by various American and more feminist forms, especially Dianic Wiccans.

Nordic Tradition

The Scandinavian countries such as Norway, Sweden and Iceland have an ancient history of earth-based spirituality, Dating back to nearly prehistoric times. The Nordic path of the Vikings has been included in this chapter because there is much misunderstood about their path.

Asatru is generally regarded with suspicion, mainly due to ties with Hitler's reign and neo-Nazism of today and Black Metal bands of the nineties and their church burnings. In *Lords of Chaos*, a book-length examination of the "Satanic" black metal music scene, authors Michael Moynihan and Didrik Sederlind look at Norwegian black metal musicians who torched some churches in 1992. The church burners' own place of worship was a small Oslo record store called Helvete, which translates, to Hell. Helvete was run by the godfather of Norwegian black metal, 0ystein Aarseth black metal to Norway with his group Mayhem.

Fortunately, more and more examples of old religions are coming out as time passes, showing an increase in awareness, and in time, an acceptance of alternative faiths. Based on the Nordic legend of *Beowulf,* Michael Creighton's book turned- film, *The Thirteenth Warrior*, centers on a Middle Eastern scholar traveling to the icy lands of Scandinavia, where he learns of Asatru beliefs. We also see the Willendorf Goddess, the stone carved figure of an ancient fertility goddess in the berserker's caverns. There exists many misleading stereotypes about Nordic paths, according to a friend of mine named Rob Crocker, who spoke to me in length on the differences between The Thule of Hitler and Nordic traditions of which he is a part. I covered much about this in my first book, *Embracing the Darkness; Understanding Dark Subcultures* wherein I spoke to both an Asatru practitioners and a few Black Metalists, who explained their beliefs well, saying "It's a mistaken correlation made by ignorant people today who can't see that the Nazi's used religion as a way to control they're own people. In the early 30s, there was a resurgence of Teutonic practices and beliefs among the folk. Those in power were able to capitalize on this and use powerful symbols like the Swastika (which is also used by Buddhists) to sway the mind of the people. Around this time there was a man named Guido Von List who through a series of visions, claimed to have discovered the essence of the runes, a system he called the Armanen system. This led to much research on Runes and since Germans did it during the rise of the Reich it is believed that Runes or any kind of Germanic religion must be evil. People tend to forget that this whole path and set of beliefs

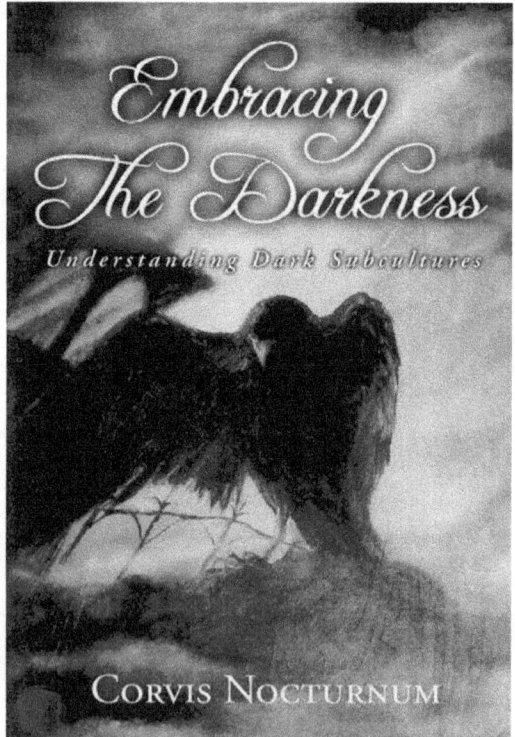

existed thousands of years before Hitler walked the earth."

Modern Heathens and Neo-Pagans as a group are tolerant, but bigots are generally not on the acceptable list. As a result, many Asatru spend a lot of time distancing themselves from the "racially aware" types. However, there is no denying there may be some connection between the appeal of the Nordic tradition and one's ancestry and heritage.

Ásatrú (Icelandic "Æsir faith") is a new religious movement which is attempting to revive the pre-Christian as described in the Eddas. It was established in the 1960s and early 1970s in Iceland, by the Íslenska Ásatrúarfélagið, which was founded by Sveinbjörn Beinteinsson. Ásatrú was recognized as an official religion by the governments of Iceland (in 1973), Denmark (in 2003) and Norway, not however in America. They respected their Gods and honored them. Perhaps they made sacrifice to give thanks or ask favor in times of danger. The Gods were more powerful then men. But they were not all-powerful, or all knowing, or entirely good. Like men, they ate, fought, played jokes, were deceived on occasion, and eventually would die. They were themselves bound by their fates, and doomed to die at the end of the world. According to Ragnorak at the end of time, even the Gods themselves die so creating this legacy of honor and truth to survive as long as possible is a powerful motivator. After which, they and the world, are to be reborn and the cycle continued.

British punks often incorporated swastika imagery and Malcolm McLaren's Sex boutique sold Nazi symbols side-by-side with S/M and fetish gear. More than just a cheap shock, the swastika deliberately mocked the ideals of the 1960s, the era of free love and flower power. This sense of despair felt by industrial culture was not unique. A similar heroic/pessimistic worldview appeared in Europe after World War I. In the early 1920s, there arose a sensibility than a movement; it fused Friedrich Nietzsche's idea of the individual will-to-power and his contempt for middle-class morality imminent downfall of the West.

It is through understanding ourselves rationally within a mystical experience do we discover the balance of both questioning and a sound mind. Too often mystics today mix theologies and new age ideas without reason and a grasp of the past, claiming it is their right to be eclectic.

In doing so, without careful research, they are often clueless of structure and a sense of order and respect for history. Above all else, the rebels of the past used some semblance of order in questioning dogma.

Chapter Six

Truth is stranger than fiction

Humanist thinkers such as Thomas Moore, Francis Bacon and Voltaire were pivotal figures in reshaping humanity's way of seeing their own lives. The most famous Humanist writer ever was Mark Twain. These men rejected Christian supernaturalism. Instead, they stressed the enjoyment of life instead of devoting life to a hereafter that required faith to believe in. Others inspired countless writers and artists of the Gothic communities from Byron, Shelly, and Goethe whose works influenced Frankenstein, vampire mythos, and the horror genre in general. We would not enjoy a good film today like *Hellraiser* or *League of Extraordinary Gentlemen*, or any of Anne Rice's books turned movies without them. Classical literature gets a tip of the hat in *The Haunting*, *The House on Haunted Hill*, and starring Brad Pitt and Morgan Freeman in *Seven*, where we see aspects of Dante's *Inferno* used by the killer.

John Milton

John Milton was born on December 9, 1608, in London. Milton's father was also a composer of church music, and Milton himself experienced a lifelong delight in music. The family's

133

financial prosperity afforded Milton to be taught classical languages, first by private tutors at home, followed by entrance to St. Paul's School at age twelve, in 1620. In 1625, Milton admitted to Christ's College, Cambridge. While Milton was a hardworking student, he was also argumentative to the extent that only a year later, in 1626, he got suspended after a dispute with his tutor, William Chappell. During his temporary return to London, Milton attended plays, and perhaps began his first forays into poetry. At his return to Cambridge, Milton was assigned a new tutor, Nathaniel Tovey. Life at Cambridge was still not easy on Milton; he felt he was disliked by many of his fellow students and he was dissatisfied with the curriculum. In April 1637, Milton was nearing the end of his studies when his mother died and was buried at Horton. Around 1632, Milton took his M.A. *cum laude* at Cambridge, after which he retired to the family homes in London and Horton, Buckinghamshire, for years of private study and literary composition. Milton arrived in Florence in the autumn, where he probably met with Galileo, then under house arrest by order of the Inquisition. In Rome, he was a guest of Cardinal Barberini, the Pope's nephew, and visited the Vatican Library. Milton's tour of

Europe was cut short with rumors of impending civil war in England, and he returned home in July 1634.

He spent his time tutoring students while finishing his life's work, the epic, *Paradise Lost*. Strangely enough, this work influenced the modern archetype of the Devil as a noble, misunderstood hero – very like Ann Rice's character Lestat, which is the likely reason Memnoch picks Lestat as his right hand man in *Memnoch the Devil*! Arguably, *Paradise Lost* is among the greatest works ever written in English. Even more remarkable for Milton's blindness — he would compose verse upon verse at night in his head and then dictate them from memory to his aides in the morning. This work contains the Devil's famous line "Better to reign in Hell than serve in Heaven" used in the old Star Trek episode which showed the eugenic superman who became better known in the film, *The Wrath of Khan*. It was a strong influence on Shelley's *Frankenstein*, as we see in the introduction were the monster in *Prometheus Unbound*, he attempts to understand humanity. The creature thinks of himself as Satan in comparison to Vicktor as

God "Evil henceforth become my good," he says. *Paradise Lost* finally saw publication in 1667, in ten books.

His funeral attended by "his learned and great Friends in London, not without a friendly concourse of the Vulgar." A monument to Milton rests in Poets' Corner at Westminster Abbey.

We'll learn more about Humanism as a philosophy in the next chapter, but Voltaire (one of the most radical of all the people spoken of previously) was a court jester in script during his day, much as is the modern song writer/singer, Voltaire, of Projekt Records is now – a snide and cynical clown in his music.

Voltaire

The original Voltaire's birth name was François-Marie Arouet de Voltaire. He was born into a middle class family, on November 21, 1694 in Paris France. He was a writer, satirist, the embodiment of the 18th-century Enlightenment, remembered as a crusader against tyranny and bigotry. Voltaire was educated

by the Jesuits at the Collège Louis-le-Grand. He studied law and then worked as a secretary to the French ambassador in Holland before devoting himself entirely to writing. He energetically attacked the government and the Catholic Church, which earned him numerous imprisonments and exiles - in 1716 Voltaire was arrested and exiled from Paris for five months. From 1717 to 1718, he found himself imprisoned in the Bastille for lampooning of the Regency. During this time, he wrote the tragedy *Edipe*, and started to use the name Voltaire. The play brought him fame but also more enemies at court. With some lucky speculation, he gained wealth in 1726.

At his 1726 stay at the Bastille, Voltaire was visited by a flow of admirers. Between 1726 and 1729, he lived in exile mainly in England. There he avoided trouble for three years and wrote in English his first essays, *Essay Upon Epic Poetry* and *Essay Upon The Civil Wars In France*, which were published in 1727. After his return to France, Voltaire wrote plays, poetry, historical and scientific treatises and became royal historiographer. The *Histoire De Charles XII* appeared in 1731 and his *Philosophical Letters* in which he compared the French system of government with the system he had seen in England, followed soon after. The book became banned and Voltaire was forced to flee Paris, but the English edition became a British bestseller.

Voltaire lived at the Château de Cirey with Madame du Châtelet in 1734-36 and 1737-40. Between those years he took refuge in Holland .From 1745 to 1750 he was a historiographer to

Louis XV and in 1746 he was elected to the French Academy but in 1750 Voltaire moved to Berlin. In 1755, he settled in Switzerland, where he lived the rest of his life, apart from trips to France. As an essayist, Voltaire defended freedom of thought and religious tolerance. His famous "I wholly disapprove of what you say, but will defend to the death your right to say it." In true Humanistic style, he believed humanity was far from its state of freedom and perfection. His *Dictionnaire Philosphique* (1764) was condemned in Paris, Geneva and Amsterdam, and for safety reasons Voltaire denied his authorship. He produced the first modern comparative history of civilizations, including Asia. An innovative aspect of Voltaire's history is that the chivalric hero is rejected for the 'good administrator', who protects liberties in order for society to prosper.

Voltaire died in Paris on May 30, 1778, at eighty-four, the undisputed leader of the Age of Enlightenment. In the Golden Age of Enlightenment, he left behind over fourteen thousand known letters and over two thousand books and pamphlets.

Goethe and Shakespearian Influence

Johann Wolfgang von Goethe, born Aug. 28, 1749, Frankfurt, Germany, died March 22, 1832, Weimar, Saxe-Weimar. Goethe was a German novelist, dramatist, poet, humanist, scientist, philosopher, and for ten years chief minister of state at Weimar.

Goethe was one of the paramount figures of German literature and European Neo-classicism and Romanticism in the late 18th and early 19th centuries. The author of *Faust* and *Theory of Colours*, he inspired Darwin with his independent discovery of the human premaxilla jawbones and focus on evolution. Goethe's influence spread across Europe, and for the next century, his works were a primary source of inspiration in music, drama, and poetry. One of the giants of world literature, Goethe was perhaps the last European to attempt the mastery and many-sidedness of the great Renaissance personalities: critic, journalist, painter, theatre manager, political leader, educationalist, natural philosopher. The bulk and diversity of his output is in itself phenomenal. His writings on science alone fill about 14 volumes. In the lyric vein, he displayed a command of a unique variety of theme and style; in the theatre his writings ranged from historical, political, or psychological plays in prose through blank-verse drama to his *Faust*, one of the masterpieces of modern literature. Goethe read the works of Shakespeare, and knew both Hegel and Schopenhauer, but did not see himself as a philosopher per se. His most notable achievement was humanizing the Devil in *Faust*, yet most of his characters were the multi faceted self-depictions of the writer. By doing so, he sought to show humanity's failings in his characters. Goethe worked others he knew into his works, such as Fredrick the Great, in the line "Who ever strives with all his power, we are allowed to save." He achieved wisdom in his 82 years of often termed Olympian, even inhuman; yet almost to the end he retained a willingness to let himself be shaken to his foundations by love or sorrow. He disciplined himself to a routine, yet he never lost the power of producing magical short lyrics in which the mystery of living, loving, and thinking was distilled into sheer transparency.

Goethe, Lord Byron, and Beethoven

Both Goethe and Byron were part of the same era. In fact, Goethe admired the cad, and he may have been an influence in the attitudes of the Devil. He admired Bach and Handel, yet his fascination was with writers mostly, not in music. Lord Byron was world famous when he became acquaintances of Goethe; at a time when being unpatriotic was near treason itself. Goethe had a dislike for most Romantics of his era, yet did not have this view of Byron. He did not fulfill the mans hopes for the future in his actions or works, yet Byron's writing *Manfred* was similar enough, yet different enough to Goethe own work to win his admiration. Ironically, Goethe didn't care for the growing preoccupation with "neo-Germanic religious-patriotic art" in fact, he felt it weak and believed music held more qualities of his liking during this time. Had he not been dead already, and Goethe had his way, Mozart would have performed the music for his play *Faust*. Goethe heard

Mozart play when he was a child, and would have loved to of had the composer perform the music for his creation *Faust*.

Deeply moved by Beethoven's music, Goethe often chided by the musician due to the fact it was not common for audiences to show approval. Goethe admired the man for his personality as well as his music. Beethoven insisted that the writer bow in public before members of the court, and caused problems by his continued disdain for the courtly niceties expected. Ludwig van Beethoven despised the monarchy, and refused to comply. Goethe did not care for Romantics much, he preferred Classical themes – no doubt, and this contributed in part to his separation from other Decadents of the day. Beethoven caused a stir in his new passionate music, unlike the style of its day. Each man came from a different mindset in his creative personality. Goethe held that restraint and limitation was a hallmark of the Classics of Greek and Roman ideals. It is ironic that a writer of Christian literature was himself pagan, owning much of his thoughts to *Homer* and *The Iliad*, yet liked Lord Byron, one of the most influential men to reshape mans' ideas on the Classics! Still, despite personal differences, Goethe admired Byron and Beethoven for life, even after they no longer spoke.

Ludwig van Beethoven

Student of a harsh instructor, young Beethoven relentlessly was pushed to be the next Mozart, court composer and child prodigy. At age ten, he filled in at church as organist and grew to be connected with many intellectual composers and performers. He dreamed of going to Vienna and eventually did. His visit was cut short by the death of his mother; a severe trauma to the young musician, for it was his mother who treated him with kindness, unlike his alcoholic father. Later he returned to Vienna and performed before Mozart, afterwards he begged to be trained by the renowned man. Mozart remarked to his friends after some time that they should keep an eye on him, as he would one day make the world notice him. His works quickly became favorites among the young Romantics, causing a ripple of commotion. The elite became very aware of his prowess, yet Beethoven himself was scornful of their attitude of pride by bloodline alone. The fiery performer blackened out Bonaparte's name after the ruler declared himself Emperor.

During middle age, his hearing began to fade rapidly. Afraid to let anyone find out, he went into hiding in the countryside at his physician's suggestion, all to no avail. He had to feel the vibrations from his piano in order to sense the notes, yet it was during this time he wrote some of his most famous works. As stated in the second chapter, Beethoven's nine symphonies (1770-1827) were divided into two groups. The first, and the third symphony was celebrating man, the fifth was about man triumphing over fate, and the seventh are vigorous, powerful and of command, representing the intellect. The second, the fourth, the sixth and the eighth are elegant, gracious and beautiful, representing the heart or intuition. They culminate in the symphony with human voices, the ninth symphony, in which the equilibrium between mind and heart. This was the "Chymical Wedding" ritual, where the Adept is born.

The beautiful majesty of Ludwig van Beethoven ended on March 26 of 1827 after he contracted a lung infection. He died during a thunderstorm, a fitting end to a man whose compositions were as rousing in passion as a storm tearing apart the sky.

Richard Wagner

Richard Wagner had a huge influence on literature and music. Inspired by Shakespeare, Dante, and Homer as well as his homeland's legends, he used his will and passion to elevate Germany's culture and status to a higher degree. Wagner saw himself, in his teens, as a man with a certain destiny, and intended to prove it to the world. Egotistical he might be, but he did indeed bring great change, even if it meant challenging the nobility. With Wagner, in his *The Twightlight of the Gods*, an opera about the Nordic Gods when Valhalla crashes down in flames. Both German composers were fiery and passionate creators, who caused a stir in their time. His life was filled with conflict and controversy by combining German archetypes and myths into operas attended by Hitler. This in part gave the dictator part of his own thoughts on using music as a method of stirring the crowds. Wagner's creations became as grand as his own ego, and doubled the musicians – a feat that has lead the modern symphony to its current size. After having the Bayreuth Opera House built (even larger than any before it), the fiery composer stepped into writing and politics, both of which were met with disfavor. It was due to this and his debts that forced him to leave Germany. He was a cheat, a liar and a womanizer, yet his contributions to music and his charisma is nearly unrivaled. He did and still draws people into his visions, and achieved a place in music history.

Percy and Mary Shelley

Percy Shelley was one of the major English romantic poets, widely considered to be among the finest lyric poets in the English language. He is perhaps most famous for such anthology pieces as *Ozymandias, Ode to the West Wind*, and *The Masque of Anarchy*; Shelley often attracted criticism and controversy for his outspoken challenges to oppression, religion, and convention as in his political poem *The Masque of Anarchy* (1819), a critical look at the Peterloo massacre, but his major works were long visionary poems such as *Adonais* and *Prometheus Unbound. "Ode To The West*

Wind" (1820) is another of Shelley's calls for revolution and change.

Shelley found friendship with fellow poets John Keats and Lord George Gordon Byron as well as paving the way for future esteemed poets such as Robert Browning, Lord Alfred Tennyson, and William Butler Yeats. His life and works are studied still and his influence lives on well into the 21st century. Shelley's unconventional life and uncompromising idealism made him a notorious and much denigrated figure in his own life, but he became the idol of the following two or three generations of poets including the major Victorian poets Robert Browning, Alfred Tennyson, Dante Gabriel Rossetti and Algernon Charles Swinburne, as well as William Butler Yeats. Young Percy entered Eton College in 1804. These six years in a conventional institution were not happy ones for Shelley, where his idealism and controversial philosophies were developing. At this time, he wrote such works as the Gothic *Zastrozzi* (1810) and *The Necessity of Atheism* (1811); "If the knowledge of a God is the most necessary, why is it not the most evident and the clearest?"

After Percy Shelley's expulsion from Oxford College for expressing his atheistic views, and now estranged from his father, he eloped with sixteen-year old Harriet Westbrook (1795-1816) to Scotland. They married on 28 August 1811 and would have two children, daughter Ianthe born in 1813 (d.1876) and son Charles born in 1814. Inviting college friend Thomas Hogg into their household, Shelley attempted an open marriage between his old friend and wife, much to the consternation of Harriet, which led to the demise of their marriage.

For the next three years, Shelley made several trips to London to the bookshop and home of William Godwin, an atheist, journalist, famous liberal philosopher and anarchic who happened to be the father of Mary Wollstonecraft Godwin – the father of Mary Shelly. She was born in London, England, the second daughter of famed feminist, educator and writer Mary Wollstonecraft.

The Shelley's were spending much time with Lord George Gordon Byron who also led a controversial life of romantic entanglements and political activity. Shelley was passionate about life and very generous to his friends, which often caused him financial hardship. They passed their days sailing on the lake and telling each other ghost stories. Mary overheard Percy and Byron speaking one night of galvanism, which inspired her most famous novel *Frankenstein; The Modern Prometheus* in 1818 within which Percy wrote the introduction. The use of Prometheus in the title was important to Shelley, but has been nearly forgotten by today's readers. Largely due to the fact, the doctor Vicktor Frankenstein was a Romantic rebel hungry for knowledge and punished for it by God for disobeying by creating life. In *Frankenstein, the Modern Prometheus* it shows that despite the fact that the "creature" only wishes to be treated as an equal, superficiality prevails. How we react to the individual affects the victim and can induce them to change into the victimizer if they lash out, thus they become the monster and the average person is to be afraid. Does society not help to create the monsters?

Erik, masked protagonist of the 1911 *Le Phantome de l'Opera* by Gaston Leroux, was much the same, save for the fact he fully accepted what he was. The newer film, starring Gerard Butler, gave a poignant depiction of a horribly scarred man with the voice and passion of an angel who also possessed the fits of rage of a cold-blooded killer. His decadent living quarters below the Opera house gave him harbor from the masses that would kill him for his hideous visage. His misanthropic nature was given birth by beatings and ridicule during childhood, and, fleeing a freak show after killing his abuser, he found peace in training the prodigal Christine. The film tries to hint at stereotypical coloring of the "hero" versus the "villains" clothing and horses, but unlike the original black and white film starring Lon Chaney, it allows full expression of range and reason for his violent passions – good and ill. We are left secretly rooting for the Phantom, well deserving, at least in part, of his vengeance. I also find some glee at the alternative ending from the original production where Lon Chaney's character was beaten to death by the angry mob. In this newer version, Butler's character survives and continues his love for the fair Christine. It is somewhat profound that this film symbolically starts in black and white, but shifts to color. A not so subtle reminder that the actions we do in the past are not easily thought of in simple terms of 'black and white'.

In 1815, the Shelly's moved back to England and settled near London. The same year Percy's grandfather died leaving him a lucrative sum (for its day) of 1000 pounds per year. The year 1816 was filled with highs and lows for Shelley, as he faced his grandfather's death, his wife Harriet drowned herself in the Serpentine River in Hyde Park, London and Mary's half sister Fanny committed suicide, but son William was born 1819 and he and Mary wed on 30 December.

Alastor or; *The Spirit of Solitude* was published in 1816 and their joint effort based on their travels *History of Six Weeks Tour* was published in 1817. Shelly praised Milton's Devil in *Paradise Lost* saying, "Nothing can exceed the energy or magnificence of the character of Satan." Not too an unusual a thought for the man married to the author of *Frankenstein*, in her own way testing the ideas of God being the only one capable of creating life in his own image. Science continued to challenge the dogma of The Church in both fact and fiction in ever-growing numbers of ways by this point in time. This is perhaps accounting for the reason for so many Goths today are Christian, Pagan, and heavy into philosophy, which will be addressed in the next chapter.

In 1818, the Shelley's moved to Italy and their son Percy Florence was born a year later. Mary was busy writing while they lived in various cities including Pisa and Rome. Percy continued to venture on sailing trips on his schooner. It sank in 1822 in a storm and Shelley drowned, at the age of twenty-nine. His body washed ashore and he was cremated on the beach. His ashes are buried in the Protestant Cemetery in Rome, Italy. The Shelley Memorial now stands at University College, Oxford, England, in honor of one of their most illustrious alumni. Ironically, the very same college expelled him earlier in life for being unchristian! The college features a white marble statue depicting Shelley as he appeared when washed ashore.

Mary Shelley died of brain cancer on February 1, 1851 in London and was interred at St. Peter's Churchyard in Bournemouth, in the English county of Dorset. At the time of her death, she was a recognized novelist after having moved back to London with her son Percy Florence. She devoted much of her time after her husband's death to compiling and publishing his works. Her fondness and respect for her husband are expressed in her extensive notes and introductions to his works contained in *The Complete Poetical Works of Percy Bysshe* in 1824. She wrote in her journal that her Faustian spirits (and her Gothic contemporaries) were "the people of the grave – that miserable conclave to which the beings I best loved belong." The selfish and hedonistic life she lead seems, later, to have lead her to morosely renounce her decadent past. Many see her work as a tale of morality, warning us not to play God without horrors befalling us, but it is one of the few works of the period that is given high regard via the literary academia, mostly due to its philosophical and medical dilemmas. Considered blasphemous in its day and long after, despite it may be seen as a religious parable in pointing out the definitive example of ambition and ego being used to break divine laws in the pursuit of science. Without it, we may not have transplants in our day which saves lives countless times.

Lord Byron

George Gordon Noel Byron was born on January 22, 1788; He was a poet and leading figure in Romanticism. Among his best-known work is *Don Juan*, which remained incomplete on his death. Byron's mark in history was not only due to his writings, but also on his life, which featured extravagant living, an unknown amount of affairs, debts and allegations of incest and sodomy.

Repellent and shocking tales of fictional and historical individuals circulated over centuries from the 1300s up to our current times. Byron himself is now considered a "grandfather" of Goth along with Poe. Byron is probably the most famous and controversial of his contemporaries. He was always a study in contrasts, a melancholy satirist, an aristocratic champion of the common person, handsome and adored but obsessed with a small personal deformity. His influence on the vampire mythos, especially in our times is evident. The fascination ingrained in peoples minds by Hollywood, brings out the surrealism and

150

feelings harkening back to Romania, where mothers told tales to misbehaving children at night to quiet them. The changes overtime have evolved from a horrific zombie lurking in shadows, to the seductive, androgynous creature of power and beauty we see today in Anne Rice's novels.

Repression during Victorian times brought out sexual fantasies in blatant form with the de Sade's writings, but vampires in books and film have lavish erotic undertones, from Stoker's female seducers of Jonathan Harker to the 1970s movie *The Vampire Lovers*, and even homosexual undertones in *Interview with a Vampire*, to outright pornography such as *Les Vampires*. The dark sensuality and allure combines sadomasochism and blood with nudity to heighten excitement. This makes it appealing to any gender or sexual orientation.

Byron's physician, Polidori, in a work of fiction, based one of the earliest incarnations of the romantic vampire off Lord Byron. The Italian, who attempted many times to become more than friends, was spurned and went back and forth in his writings from love to hate. This was no doubt part of the early ambiguous sexual leanings that vampires have always exuded, in both males and females alike, from then till now.

Byron fled England to escape scandal and a failed marriage and died of fever in 1824. His natural gift for poetry was the only consistency in his troubled life. Yet even during his lifetime, his personal life overshadowed his work. He was famously described by Lady Caroline Lamb as "mad, bad, and dangerous to know."

Promethean Flame by Corvis Nocturnum
Charles Baudelaire

Charles Baudelaire was a 19th century Decadent. The French poet, translator, and literary and art critic whose reputation rests primarily on *Les Fleurs du mal, The Flowers of Evil* which was perhaps the most important and influential poetry collection published in Europe in the 19th century. Similarly, his 1868 *Little Prose Poems* was the most successful and innovative early experiment in prose poetry of the time. Known for his controversial and often dark poetry, as well as his translation of the tales of Edgar Allan Poe, Baudelaire's life was filled with drama and anguish, mostly due to financial problems while being prosecuted for his works deemed as obscenity and blasphemy. He was quoted as saying once "all literature is the consequence of sin."

In his often-introspective poetry, Baudelaire revealed himself as a seeker of God without religious beliefs, and sought every manifestation of life for some kind of true significance. Like the gloomier Poe, Baudelaire crafted works mixing decay with beauty, in true Gothic style showing in death to be the reason to cherish life – the reason why antiquity Goths of the 1980's and 90's were originally called New Decadents, long before renaming themselves "Goths."

Baudelaire began his education at the Collège Royal in Lyons. It was during this time that Baudelaire began to show promise as a student and a writer. Intense melancholy also developed and the poet was expelled in 1839 from school due to his consistent acts of indiscipline.

Eventually Baudelaire became a nominal student of while living a "free life" in the Latin Quarter, where he made his first contacts in the literary world, and contracted the venereal disease that eventually would take his life. Baudelaire jumped a ship in Mauritius and eventually made his way back to France in February of 1842. The voyage and his exploits after jumping the ship enriched his imagination, and brought a rich mixture of exotic images to his works.

Baudelaire received an inheritance the same year and rapidly proceeded to dissipate it on the lifestyle of a true gothic dandy, spending freely on the finest clothes, books, works of art, expensive food and wines, and, as rumor has it, opium. Shortly after returning from the South Seas, Baudelaire met the mulatto woman known as Jeanne Duval, who, first as his mistress and then, after the mid-1850s, as his financial charge, was to dominate his life for the next 20 years. Her presence would inspire Baudelaire's sensual love poetry, her magnificent flowing black hair giving him inspiration for such masterpieces of erotica in *La Chevelure*, which translates to "The Head of Hair".

Baudelaire's extravagance exhausted half his fortune in less than two years, and he fell prey to moneylenders, thus laying the foundation for huge debts that would haunt him for the rest of his life. His family levied on him a legal arrangement that restricted his access to his inheritance. This in turn made him legally a minor. The minuscule allowance barely granted him enough to clear his debts causing him emotional and financial dependence on his mother while increasing his growing resentment for his stepfather. The moods of isolation and despair that Baudelaire had known in adolescence became more frequent. He remains to this day a renowned poet and critic.

William Blake

William Blake was a bit of a late Renaissance man, though largely ignored during his lifetime. Born in London in 1757, he was a pioneer in the Decadent period, around the same time as Sir Francis Dashwood. He was a poet, artist, a visionary mystic and engraver (who illustrated and printed his own books, centuries before vanity press existed in its current form!) Blake is important to note among writers linked to esoteric thinkers as he used mysticism as inspiration in his work, despite the fact he proclaimed the supremacy of the imagination over the rationalism of the 18th- century. Misunderstanding dogged his career as a writer and artist. It was not until generations passed until many

154

would recognize his importance - I recently ran across his name in Anne Rice's *Memnoch the Devil*, were the statue of a fallen angel was said to resemble that of Blake's artwork. In 1767, he was sent to Henry Pars' drawing school. Blake has recorded that from his early years, he experienced visions of angels (while sitting nude in a treetop as a youth) and ghostly monks He claimed to have seen and conversed with the angel Gabriel, the Virgin Mary, and various historical figures. No doubt, that fact influenced Rice's use of his name. Blake said of Milton "he was a true Poet and of the Devil's party without knowing it."

At the age of 14, Blake apprenticed for several years to an engraver, and his work became influenced further by Gothic art and architecture. Blake's first book of poems, *Poetical Sketches*, appeared in 1783 and followed it by *Songs of Innocence* some time later. Interestingly I discovered that Allen Ginsberg nearly convinced Mick Jagger to redo this work in a song, according to Gavin Baddeley's research in *Lucifer Rising*. Apparently, The Rolling Stones' interest in the occultists such as Levi, Decadent poets and The Marquis de Sade as well as inspiration from other sinister icons shows up in much of their works. In the ending of the Rice film *Interview with the Vampire*, the song *Sympathy for the Devil*, is an obvious tribute to the Stones version by Guns and Roses singer Axel Rose. The anti-hero connection of the Decadents once again is subtly felt once more mixing the anti-hero vampire archetype with Milton's Devil.

In *Songs of Innocence,* the world is seen from a child's point of view, but they also function as tales relevant to the adult experience. Blake engraved and published most of his major works himself. Famous among his *Prophetic Books* are *The Book of Thel, The Marriage of Heaven and Hell, The Book of Urizen, America, Milton,* and *Jerusalem.* In his *Prophetic Books,* Blake expressed his constant concern with the struggle of the soul to free its "natural energies from reason and organized religion". Among Blake's later art works are drawings and engravings for Dante's *Divine Comedy* that did not see completion until he was nearly 70 years old.

Blake died on August 12, 1827, and was buried in an unmarked grave in a public cemetery. Though generally thought of as an eccentric during his own life, as time passed he is highly rated as both a poet and artist.

Writers throughout the age's poets and novelists have created outlets for others in reading their works or inspiring them to follow their example. The television show *Beauty and the Beast,* starring Linda Hamilton and Ron Perlman was a favorite of mine when I was younger due to the fact I sympathized with Vincent, the "beast" character, being a creative, quiet and introspective youth, and found within him qualities that mirrored my own. He was a poet, I an artist. I also related to his feelings of distance from the rest of my peers. "I have seen your world. It has no place for me," he tells her, "I remind them of what they fear the most…their aloneness." Introspection of feelings, from within and observing

156

those of others around them gives us pause for thought. Nietzsche stated, "The best and highest that men can acquire they must attain by crime." This leads one to think that only by ignoring the laws of man can we have our justice, regardless of the monster it makes us. In the 2006 release *V for Vendetta*, we have another anti-hero who, while also horribly scarred internally as well as externally, fights the system, conformity and the oppression of dogmatic dictatorship and maintains a love of beauty, creativity and freedom. Often it is the underdog, like Shelley's Frankenstein, that challenges us the most because even if we fail to see it as a tale of morality versus control over our fellow man, religion versus science, we still subliminally understand the underlying meaning. A tongue in cheek movie like it was *Frankenweenie* and *Vincent*, both early works by Tim Burton. His *Edward Scissor hands* propelled him to a career full of movies challenging the stagnant complacency of most people.

Films that challenged the concept of 'Good' versus 'evil', taking the side of the anti-hero, began to emerge, gradually reshaping modern public opinion on many things, from justice to sexuality. However, sexuality challenging the status quo has been with us for some time, with one of the most obvious literary figures being the Marquis de Sade.

Marquis de Sade

About the Marquis de Sade, everyone knows too much, and too little. Even during his own lifetime, the myth of de Sade was growing, taking on a shape of its own, larger than his own life, so that he came to live not just behind the stonewalls of the Bastille, but behind an equally impenetrable mask of false notions perpetuated by other people. In the end, he became a being not entirely of himself, but rather a kind of collaborative construction. A being of myth, a force in the consciousness of humanity, known by only one name: 'de Sade."

"I wanted only to try to live in accord with the promptings which came from my true self. Why was that so very difficult?"
~The Marquis De Sade

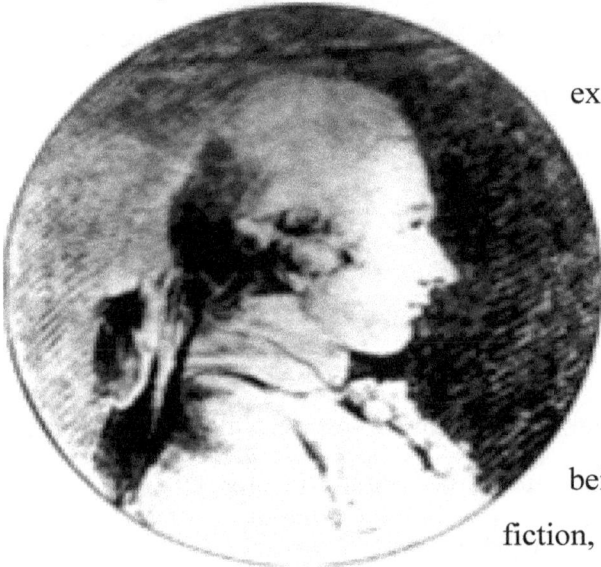

Even stripped of exaggerations, de Sade's real life was as dramatic and as tragic as a cautionary tale. There is much to the saying about truth being stranger than fiction, but the Marquis de Sade wrote, "Truth titillates the imagination far less than fiction." Certainly, de Sade was in a position to speak knowledgeably about both imagination and titillation, although his ability to distinguish between truth and fiction is a little less apparent.

Donatien Alphonse François Comte de Sade was born into privileged French nobility in 1740. A spoiled child, he grew up on various country estates, including an ancient castle with a Dank, miserable dungeon, which no doubt played a factor in his developing psyche. He was also the subject of a Catholic school education. Unlike the current Catholic school setup, in which youngsters are subjected to mostly mental abuse and molestation, the Jesuits of the day included public whippings as part of the daily routine. He often speculated that everyone indulged as he did, just more quietly. Writing later in life, he said, "So long as the laws remain such as they are today, employ some discretion: loud opinion forces us to do so; but in privacy and silence let us compensate ourselves for that cruel chastity we are obliged to display in public."

He was married (against his wishes) to a middle-class heiress for money, and caused scandals with prostitutes. He enjoyed orgies blasphemy and subversion in equal measure. Within months of his marriage, he was arrested for mixing those pleasures. De Sade invited a prostitute over for what at first appeared to be the usual procedure, but quickly diverted from foreplay into, well, something else. According to the woman, Sade masturbated into a chalice, called God a "motherfucker" and inserted communion hosts into her "naughty bits," all the while screaming for God to strike him down if He was so tough.

De Sade was sentenced to the first of what would be many stints in prison. After a few months, he was released to exile outside Paris, the equivalent of house arrest. Under close surveillance from the authorities, he returned to debauchery—albeit apparently without the aid of religious artifacts—and with his sister-in-law. This enraged his mother in- law, who had him imprisoned under a *lettre de cachet* for 14 years until the Revolution freed him. To pass the time in prison, he secretly began scratching out writings, which he wisely concealed from his jailers. The ex-marquis became a Revolutionary, miraculously escaping the guillotine during the Terror, only to be arrested later for publishing his erotic novels. He spent his final 12 years in the insane asylum at Charenton, where he caused yet another scandal by directing plays using inmates and professional actors. Ironically, his jailers practiced his ideas, and the asylum sold his writings in attempt to avoid bankruptcy. De Sade died at the asylum in 1814, virtually in the arms of his teenage mistress.

De Sade didn't think he had done anything wrong. In a letter written from prison, he said, "Man's natural character is to imitate; that of the sensitive man is to resemble as closely as possible the person whom he loves. It is only by imitating the vices of others that I have earned my misfortunes." It's hard to imagine which "others" de Sade could have been imitating. Between his squalid surroundings and his even more squalid brain, the Marquis produced exactly the kind of writing you would expect. Horrific. His writing features the sum total of bad things that people can do to other people, including rape, necrophilia, oral sex, sodomy, incest, and gang bangs. Suffice to say, the Marquis, no matter how depraved, had hit upon a few gems of wisdom during his disturbed life. "Wolves which batten upon lambs, lambs consumed by wolves, the strong who immolate the weak, the weak victims of the

160

strong: there you have Nature, there you have her intentions, there you have her scheme: a perpetual action and reaction, a host of vices, a host of virtues, in one word, a perfect equilibrium resulting from the equality of good and evil on earth."

Current Ties

Many of the activities that de Sade practiced are a part of the BDSM scene today, in one form or another, although some are avoided due to legal issues or personal conscience. "Without limits, our actions would have no naughtiness," argues de Sade. By and large, BDSM is illegal as it consists of restraint, beatings and sodomy, a crime still on the books in most states. However, fantasy and putting it into action still exist. It is the heartbeat of fantasy and eroticism that is the lifeblood of the porn industry, of sex shops that have existed through time in one way or another. From *The Kama Sutra* to Hooters restaurants, sex will always be a primary pursuit of humanity, regardless of the fanatic repression by prudish government lobbyists and religious fundamentalists. We have religions and laws aplenty that dictate our actions, stifling our creative freedom by dictating what is acceptable, which causes guilt in healthy relationships sexually. The Marquis de Sade made a career telling tales of unrepressed urges taken to extremes. Labeled a monster in history as well as now, he nonetheless is devoured by his audiences through the passing decades. Is *the Shadow* that Jung spoke of evident here? Is the Marquis evil by bringing up hidden desires found in people, or is he just more able to articulate the thought suppressed by religious puritanical

161

thought? Research shows that art and entertainment enhance life, not adversely affect it. If not, if such monsters and figures historically were not of some value for study, would they have gained the attention they have? It is important to take a close look at ourselves, to be healthy, regardless of guilt. Religion was hardly foremost in the Marques mind save when he said in Justine, "God is what interests us least." He saw argument in Adam in Milton's Paradise Lost, saying ignorance of vice and of its temptations permits only a blank for virtues and that Adam himself is a puppet. As he says to the libertines in the world in *Philosophy in the Boudoir*, "Voluptuaries of all ages, of every sex, it is to you only that I offer this work; nourish yourselves upon its passions..." Unlike Emily Dickenson's poetic persona, de Sade exploited his imagination, inverting anything of virtue, especially Christian virtue, in part to ridicule the prudishness and repression of his Day. During the heights of Prohibition, alcohol flourished in America in the speakeasies as my grandmother said. It is when we are told not to do something we as people want to explore it the most. The curiosity of our minds is that of Pandora, opening the Box. True, it does lend its miseries upon us; such actions can enlighten and expand us. De Sade, his writings and his overall attitude, (tempered with personal responsibility due to rampant diseases to be avoided) is part of the modern Satanist on sexuality. Not to mention Satanists only have willing partners, unlike de Sade and his escapades!

Modern critics have rightly pointed out that de Sade foreshadowed the age of psychoanalysis, identifying the power and the nature of the sexual obsessions that would later be more clinically obsessed over by Sigmund Freud. Ironically, it takes one mad man to understand another. de Sade himself wrote, "Lust is to the other passions what the nervous fluid is to life; it supports them all, lends strength to them all... ambition, cruelty, avarice, revenge, are all founded on lust."

Nietzschean philosophers have studied de Sade, seeking to liberate physical, moral, and spiritual nihilism – the end of all things in a state of nihilism, in a nearly sacred destruction of excess, like Nietzsche's cult of Dionysus. The musician Marilyn Manson was a Goth shock rocker who loved both classical thinkers, and his devoted followers could consider him to be similar due to his lyrics and stage antics. These people show us the logical extremes of repression on a society and the severe backlash that can be found. The core of our culture, nature and society have always had atrocities, long before and after de Sade, Anton LaVey and others that have been deemed evil. Nations have committed unspeakable acts on neighboring nations and will always do so. Ironic that the world picks thinkers bold enough to say what is obvious to all, and scapegoat them for simply speaking up what is on the minds of so many. Such rationalism is the bedrock of humans attempt to explore, to understand others and ourselves. The human mind is a fragile thing. Some might say that by being criminal (locked away for thirty years) and mentally unstable, it

163

makes De Sade a more striking character. Prohibitions on crime and violence add to the irrational person's actions, such as serial killers, sadistic rapists. According to the philosopher Hegel's terms, transgression should not be confused with reversion to a "state of nature.' Transgression in the mind of de Sade here is in the ego of the depraved writer himself. His frenzy and ecstasy match Hyde's "undignified pleasures" in Robert Luis Stevenson's writings. It could be debated that de Sade, Stevenson, Nietzsche, and Marilyn Manson all were living examples of their belief that man on Earth was a state of decline, in which the world itself was decaying by our own actions, collectively. As Einstein's work was used for evil in the destruction of countless innocents in Japan. It also can be harnessed for good, as in fuel for cities in nuclear reactors aiding humankind. With an appetite of perversion, blasphemy and in holding up a mirror to ourselves, they offer us a chance to see extremes of humanity without testing the waters ourselves, they delight in poking holes at morality, and the haughtiness of the dogmatic thinkers.

After decade upon decade of research, study reveals an astonishingly non-sadistic de Sade, his capacity for deep romantic love, his inexhaustible charm, his delusional paranoia. Through a dazzling reading of de Sade's novels, including the notorious masterpiece *120 Days of Sodom*, many now argue powerfully for Sade as one of the great literary imaginations of the eighteenth century. Many films have been made, up to Gregory Rush playing the part in *Quills,* depicting him as a poetic philosopher, albeit a perverted one. The Promethean and Faustian qualities of de Sade and others, such as Johnny Depp's character in *The Libertine*, makes sad anti-heroes out of those who would dare truly be 'free.' Since the days of Plato and Aristotle the discussion of crime and evil in art have long been debated. What de Sade, and others, may truly be saying is that normal social beings cannot accept that they resonate the same forgotten truths of our forefathers who challenged the world before them.

Chapter Seven

Waxing philosophical

We have examined occultism, secret societies, early scientists and writers who shaped the world over time. The quest for knowledge beyond dogma is reflective throughout time, from the Templars and the Masons to the Illuminati. The majority of these radicals were students of philosophy as well, and we see it in fiction of the past and in sci-fi fiction of today. In works such as Humanist Gene Roddenberry's Star Trek we see traits of Prometheus. Roddenberry wrote in fiction what was far before his time – which dealt with freedoms and anti-racism concepts. Bear in mind the sixties when race riots raged in schools, he depicted interracial (and alien relationships), as well as scientific marvels we are now beginning to see today with cloning, bluetooth technology and PDA's (tiny ear bud cell phones and personal Data assistants, which resemble communicators and other devices on every Star Trek spin off). This is as much a part of freedom from control found in Shelley's work. Horror can be an exploration of the psyche of man – what separates us from the monsters is often a fine line. We dream, we explore, and create. If God, in such tales, was not alone on having held the keys for life itself, did that not place man on more of a level with Nature than fighting against it for survival? This core belief is the heart of existential metaphysics and philosophy. The plethora of so called "sacred cows" we learn about in most schools and churches are challenged more and more every decade and every passing day for greater understanding. If we did not ask questions, as Galileo and Newton did before us we would not have advanced out of the mental and spiritual darkness of the Dark Ages. The father of philosophy, Aristotle, once remarked "Everyone adheres to a philosophy whether they are aware of it or not." All of us have patterns to our lives; behaviors that guide our lives and help us cope with the stress of life. It is through our attempts to examine how we perceive the world around us. Plato observed philosophy covers the entire range of human thought and activity as well as science, economics, and government. It is how history is recorded, especially in a social context. Art, literature, are expressions of how we react in and because of the world – truly art imitates life, and vice versa. In tracing the beginnings of philosophers, we must seek our answers in the past, in Greek and Roman times.

Aristotle

Aristotle was an ancient Greek philosopher and student of Plato. Along with Plato and Socrates, Aristotle is considered one of the most influential of ancient Greek philosophers. As we will discover, philosophy shaped man's thoughts as well as politics. Bear in mind, the early Roman Empire was the first Republic. Anyone who read of Shakespeare's *Caesar* in high school will

remember that the Senate and the ruling head is similar to most countries way of government. Our system in America is based off the Republic of ancient Rome and Benjamin Franklin's dealings with the five-civilized tribes of American Indians merged with his sense of brotherhood via the Freemasonry ideals that gave birth to our system of self-regulation. They transformed Pre-Socratic Greek philosophy into the foundations of Western philosophy as we know it - the writings of Plato (*Plato's Republic*) and Aristotle form the core of ancient philosophy. His philosophical works including *The Categories*, which is his examines of the definition of the terms used in the process of logic and reasoning.

Whereas Plato said that the universal is found *separately from* things, the third of the three main Greek philosophers, Aristotle developed his own philosophy in deductive logic, trying to bring order to chaos; "the science of the universal essence of that which is actual." That being, reality, in the realm of the physical, is acquired through experience that the universal is found *within* things. However, only a small percentage of the Aristotelian writings have survived, and many appear as works in progress. His meticulous studies and teachings in such topics as aesthetics, biology, ethics, government, logic, morality, and physics greatly influenced Western philosophical and scientific thought.

Born in 384 BC, Aristotle was the son of Nichomachus, a court physician to King Amyntas of Macedonia. After his father's death, his uncle became his guardian, and sent him to study in Athens. For almost twenty years, Aristotle studied then taught Philosophy at the Academy under Plato who in turn had been taught by Socrates.

An accomplished student, Aristotle often disagreed with his teacher and after Plato's death in 347; Aristotle parted ways with the Platonic teachings. His extensive study and classification of animals into *genera* and *species* for example, expressed in such works as *On the Parts of Animals* and *The History of Animals* (350 BCE) have contributed greatly to the modern study of biology. With growing anti Macedonian sentiments, Aristotle left Athens. He wrote books on many subjects, including physics, poetry, zoology, logic, rhetoric, government, and biology.

Aristotle is known for being one of the few figures in history who studied almost every subject possible at the time. In science, Aristotle studied anatomy, astronomy, economics, embryology, geography, geology, meteorology, physics, and zoology. In philosophy, Aristotle wrote on aesthetics, ethics, government, metaphysics, politics, psychology, rhetoric and theology. He also dealt with education, foreign customs, literature and poetry. His combined works practically constitute an encyclopedia of Greek knowledge. Aristotle was the teacher of legendary Alexander the Great, born in Pella, Macedon, and King of Macedon during 336–323 BCE. Alexander is considered one of the most successful military commanders in world history, conquering most of the known world before his death. His conquests ushered in centuries of Greek settlement and rule over foreign areas, a period known as the Hellenistic Age. Alexander himself lived on in the history and myth of both Greek and non-Greek cultures. Already during his lifetime, and especially after his death in June of 323 BCE, his exploits inspired a literary tradition in which he appears as a towering legendary hero in the tradition of Achilles.

As Athens was rebelling against Macedonian rule imposed after the death of Alexander the Great, Aristotle's life was in peril because of his political ties, so he fled to the island of Euboea. He died soon after at his home in Chalcis, Euboea, 322 BCE at the age of sixty-two years. Aristotle believed in the eternal nature of the universe with no beginning and no end; "It is not once nor twice but times without number that the same ideas make their appearance in the world."- *On the Heavens.*

Aristotle wrote about human nature in one of lesser-read works of Aristotle, *Rhetoric,* and *Book one*: "The motives that make men do wrong to others; we are next to consider the states of mind in which they do it, and the persons to whom they do it. They must themselves suppose that the thing can be done, and done by them: either that they can do it without being found out, or that if they are found out they can escape being punished, or that if they are punished the disadvantage will be less than the gain for themselves or those they care for. The general subject of apparent possibility and impossibility will be handled later on, since it is relevant not only to forensic but to all kinds of speaking. But it may here be said that people think that they can themselves most easily do wrong to others without being punished for it if they possess eloquence, or practical ability, or much legal experience, or a large body of friends, or a great deal of money. Their confidence is greatest if they personally possess the advantages mentioned: but even without them they are satisfied if they have friends or supporters or partners who do possess them: they can thus both commit their crimes and escape being found out and punished for committing them. They are also safe, they think, if they are on good terms with their victims or with the judges who try them. Their victims will in that case not be on their guard against being wronged, and will make some arrangement with them instead of prosecuting; while their judges will favour them because they like them, either letting them off altogether or imposing light sentences. They are not likely to be found out if their appearance contradicts the charges that might be brought against them: for instance, a weakling is unlikely to be charged with violent assault, or a poor and ugly man with adultery. Public and open injuries are the easiest to do, because nobody could at all suppose them possible, and therefore no precautions are taken. The same is true of crimes so great and terrible that no man living could be suspected of them: here too no precautions are taken. For all men guard against ordinary offences, just as they guard against ordinary diseases; but no one takes precautions against a disease that nobody has ever had. You feel safe, too, if you have either no enemies or a great many; if you have none, you expect not to be watched and therefore not to be detected; if you have a great many, you will be watched, and therefore people will think you can never risk an attempt on them, and you can defend your innocence by pointing out that you could never have taken such a risk. You may also trust to hide your crime by the way you do it or the place you do it in, or by some convenient means of disposal."

The above, then, are the various states of mind in which a man sets about doing wrong to others. Truly, little has changed since then. In his research of the earth sciences such as Meteorology (350 BC), Aristotle discusses his findings in climactic activity such as thunderstorms, rainbows, and beyond to meteors and the Milky Way. In honor of his contribution to the studies of the heavens, a lunar crater is now named after him.

Humanism.

Philosophy has its infancy in the ancient Greek and Roman civilization, with Humanism, possibly being the largest group of philosophers holding these ideals. According to the American

173

Humanist Association "Humanism is a progressive philosophy of life that, without supernaturalism, affirms our ability and responsibility to lead ethical lives of personal fulfillment that aspire to the greater good of humanity." Based strongly on the works of Plato, Aristotle and others after it entails a search for truth and morality through human-interest.

Humanists reject the supernatural and dependency on faith, feeling morality is based on common sense, with cause and effect rather than from religion. To understand how this came about, we must trace the roots of philosophy itself. Tyranny and ignorance was the enemy of Masons and Humanists alike. Even the founding fathers, which most believe today were righteous "God fearing" men, we find the mixture of Paganism and Christianity via the Masons like Washington and Deists like Benjamin Franklin, Thomas Paine. The lines between science and theology become farther apart. The efficiency of prayer and divine miracles become dimmer. Franklin, known for his quote, "god helps those who helps those that help themselves," has more of a slant of man being foremost, his spirituality second.

Galileo and the Renaissance

Humanism during the 17th and eighteenth century caused a stir while being ruled over by both the Monarchy and the Roman Catholic Church, which ruled central Europe. The people responsible for the Illuminati were the early scientists, as we learned in the first half of this book. The affects of social, cultural, and political movement due to Humanism grew. The revival of

Latin, Greek and Roman languages, and art caused philosophy and science to explode. This revival was based on interpretations on art and much more, making strides from the contemplation that the Bible held all the answers. Values, such as meekness and humility weakened by key figures, and Humanism became branded as "a dangerous doctrine." The wealthy came to feel being educated on classical Greek and Roman mythos, music, and entertained by plays were the hallmarks of being regal, that they deserved culture above the rabble in the streets below their ivory towers. This rift increased between the "haves and the have nots", and we see more of it as time passed into the Shakespearian era.

In Italy, the Medici family was no doubt most influential in aiding this stir, for the family was a huge patron of the arts, and occultism, as we saw in chapter two and three. During this time, Galileo upheld Copernicus theory that the Earth was not central to the Universe. The discipline of science we know today did not exist. The Pope requested Galileo cease teaching such blasphemous ideas. Flatly refusing, he published *Dialogsvs De Systemate,* containing ridicule of the Pope. Later, during his trail, he was forced to deny many ideas. Bitter Galileo's problems continued during the Spanish Inquisition.

As mentioned in part one, Newton felt God's only reason for existence was to tinker with the minute adjustments of stars. Mathematicians did not account for comets during his time; they were oddities in the sky. Newton and his fellow deists held there was no divine intervention in the order of Nature, that it was a self-regulating machine.

One of the earliest contemporary humanist organizations was the Humanistic Religious Association of London in 1853. With democratically led elections, this group of both male and female members promoted sciences, philosophy and all the arts.

Dualism

Dualism of one form or another has always existed as a safe haven for supernatural religions the world over. Immanuel Kant, as we will see later on, dashed to fragments the idea using logic the rational arguments for God, yet established them in terms of a super naturalistic demand of man's faith. Philosophers like Hegel, Kant and more all echo Desecrates famous statement "I think, therefore I am," to new levels over the next 300 years.

The Key Points

One of Humanism central ideas is that it rejects theistic religious belief and the existence of a supernatural. It is often associated with scientists and academics, although it is not at all limited to these groups. Secular humanists generally believe that following humanist principles naturally leads to secularism, on the basis that religious views cannot be supported rationally. Humanists have their roots in Greek and Rome, and have expressed themselves vividly in Queen Elizabeth's' day, as well as Franklins', but mostly it is the idea that man is the center of the universe, not a particle of it. The ten key points of Humanism today is a belief in natural metaphysics, and that the supernatural is a myth. Nature is the totality of being, with matter and energy existing independently of a higher conscious.

Second, they draw on the laws and facts of science, thinking man is an evolution of nature and a part of it, without consciousness after death.

Third, Humanism believes man possess the power to solve their own problems, relying on reason and scientific method.

Fourth, it opposes predestination, fatalism, and embraces life with the opinion that they control their own destiny.

Fifth, they believe in ethics and morality that ground all human value in our earthly experience – with man's highest goal being happiness, freedom, and cultural/economic freedom.

Sixth, they feel individuals attain their life's maximum benefit by combining personal satisfaction with the betterment of society.

Seventh, a belief in the widest expanse in art and nature's beauty.

Eighth, the desire to uphold far reaching social programs enhancing democracy and peace.

Ninth, implementing scientific reason with government and cultural life.

Lastly, Humanism believes questioning convictions in all things. They take the stance that humanity has not reached the height of its full potential, as indeed, it may never. We must find our destiny in the here and now. As Judeo-Christianity loses its grip on every aspect of civilized life, we seek answers elsewhere.

Over fifty percent of all people on the face of the Earth are not Christian, it may seem odd that while Classical artists such as Rapheal, Leonardo, and Michelangelo used Christian themes, they used color, form, and Pagan elements, expressing the wide range of humanities possibilities. The poets and writers such as Shakespeare all implemented Humanist ideas – as found in Hamlet, where it states' "What a piece of work is man! How noble in reason!" As mentioned previously, Voltaire was a Humanist, saying once that "people will not truly be free until the last emperor is hung from the entrails of the last priest," clearly rejecting the Church and Monarchy of his day. Humanist of the Reniassance were hand in hand with the secret societies mentioned in the first half. Later on in Europe, especially Germany, philosophy became even more prominent in a world view, without fear of reprisal by a crowned prince.

Schopenhauer

Among nineteenth century philosophers, Arthur Schopenhauer was among the first to contend that the universe is hardly a rational place. He developed philosophy by emphasizing that in the face of what he believed to be a world filled with endless strife, we should minimize desires in order to achieve a more tranquil frame of mind and a disposition towards everything. Often considered to be a pessimist, Schopenhauer actually advocated artistic forms of awareness to overcome what he considered to be a painful human condition. As such philosophy has had a special attraction for those engaged in music, literature, and the arts.

At age nineteen Arthur Schopenhauer left for college. His mother developed a strong friendship with Goethe who became a writer himself. The young Schopenhauer turned from medicine to philosophy. By now heavy into the works of Plato and Kant, and during the years of 1814-1818 he began *The World as Will and Representation.* He studied panentheism (all in God) opposed to pantheism (all is God), which is what we comprehend and image to be the universe, is an aspect of God, but that the being God is a projection we can imagine.

In March of 1820 Hegel went to Berlin and Schopenhauer decided to hold a class at the same time as the more popular lecturer. Unfortunately for him, no students turned up to Schopenhauer's course of lectures, and subsequently he left, never to teach in a university again. He commented on his rival, "The height of audacity in serving up pure nonsense, in stringing together senseless and extravagant mazes of words, such as had in madhouses, was finally reached in Hegel...a monument to Germany." Ironically, his theories proved to be equally as difficult to explain. In 1831 a cholera epidemic broke out in Berlin and both Hegel and Schopenhauer fled; but Hegel returned prematurely, caught the infection, and died a few days later. Schopenhauer called himself a Kantian and despised Hegel. He formulated a pessimistic philosophy that gained importance and support after the failure of the German and Austrian revolutions. Although he seemed to be pessimistic, it was Schopenhauer who spoke the famous words, "Eat, drink, and be merry, for tomorrow we die," it could be viewed either way. Schopenhauer took Kant's division of the universe claiming that the Will was the driving force of the world. For Schopenhauer, human will had sway over the intellect. This idea was rare among philosophers in considering logic less important than art, and certain forms of religious discipline; Schopenhauer concluded that discursive thought like philosophy and logic did not affect the nature of desire, the Will. In *The World as Will* and *Representation*, Schopenhauer wrote that humans living in the realm of objects are living in the realm of desire, and thus are eternally tormented by that desire - his idea of the role of desire in life is similar to that of Hinduism and Buddhism ideals.

Schopenhauer differed from Immanuel Kant, who felt things became solid in our minds. Schopenhauer felt we knew our own bodies better than anything else. People take up space, have needs and desires – which is what he termed "Will." People suffer, feel, and want involuntarily. Schopenhauer didn't think love was a part of us by accident, and that we understand it to be a powerful force in our psyche which shaped the whole world. Schopenhauer believed one way to escape the suffering inherent in a world of Will was through art, that "music was the only art that did not merely copy ideas, but actually embodied the will itself." Further, Schopenhauer additionally maintained a marked metaphysical and politically unchristian way of thinking. He argued that Christianity constituted a revolt against the materialistic basis of Judaism, exhibiting an Indian-influenced ethics reflecting the Aryan theme of spiritual "self-conquest" as opposed to "the ignorant drive toward earthly utopianism of the superficially" on Earth. He was strongly against taboos on issues like suicide and masochism and condemned the treatment of African slavery. Schopenhauer's works influenced the ideas and writings of Nietzsche, Sigmund Freud and Carl Jung. Nietzsche more than likely followed Schopenhauer's ideas in regarding the Will as the heart of all things – in the self being most highly regarded aspect of anything. A far cry indeed from the meek and pious monks of the Dark Ages.

George Wilhelm Friedrich Hegel

Along with Nietzsche, Hegel (1770-1831) belongs to the period of "German idealism" in the decades following Kant. The most systematic of the post-Kantian idealists, Hegel attempted to elaborate a comprehensive and systematic "logical" starting point. He is perhaps most well-known for his ideas of history, an account which was later taken over by Marx and "inverted" or perverted, into a materialist theory of historical development culminating in communism. For most of the twentieth century, the "logical" side of Hegel's thought had been largely forgotten, but his political and social philosophy continued to find support.

After graduation Hegel worked as a tutor for various families until around 1800. Hegel devoted himself to developing his ideas on religious and social themes, and saw himself as a type of modernizing and reforming educator. In 1801, he moved to the University of Jena, which had become a centre of both "Kantian" philosophy and the early Romantic Movement. In 1801, Hegel published his first philosophical work, *The Difference between Fichte's and Schelling's System of Philosophy.* By late 1806, Hegel had completed his first major work, the *Phenomenology of Spirit.*

The occupation of Jena by Napoleon's troops as Hegel was completing the manuscript closed the university and Hegel left the town. Now without a university appointment he worked for a short time, apparently very successfully, as an editor of a newspaper in Bamberg, and then from 1808-1815 as the headmaster and philosophy teacher in Nuremberg. During this time, he wrote and published his *Science of Logic.* In 1816, he managed to return to his university career by being appointed to a chair in philosophy at the University of Heidelberg. Then in 1818, he was offered and took up the chair of philosophy at the University of Berlin, the most prestigious position in the German philosophical world. In 1821 in Berlin Hegel published his major work in political philosophy, *Elements of the Philosophy of Right*, based on lectures dealing with "objective spirit." During the following ten years, up to his death in 1831, Hegel enjoyed celebrity at Berlin, and published subsequent versions of the Encyclopedia. After his death, versions of his lectures on philosophy of history, philosophy of religion, aesthetics, and the history of philosophy became published.

During his stay in Berlin, important forms of later critical reaction to Hegelian philosophy developed. Hegel had been a supporter of progressive but non-revolutionary politics, but his followers divided into "left-" and "right-wing" factions; from out of the former circle, Karl Marx was to develop his own approach to society and history which appropriated many Hegelian ideas into Marx's materialistic outlook. The Communistic Soviet versions of Marxism, many "Marxists" incorporated further Hegelian elements back into their forms of Marxist philosophy. Many of the criticisms of Hegel's rationalism found their way into subsequent "existentialist" thought, which we'll see later via Ayn Rand.

In academic philosophy, Hegelian idealism underwent a revival in both Great Britain and the United States in the last decades of the nineteenth century. In Britain, as well as America, metaphysical ideas came to be one of the main targets of attack by the founders of the "analytic" movement; with revolutionary innovations in logic starting in the last decades of the nineteenth century had destroyed Hegel's metaphysics by overturning the Aristotelian logic on which it was based. Hegel nevertheless continued to be a figure of interest within other philosophical movements such as existentialism and Marxism. In the 1960s, the German philosopher Klaus Hartmann developed what was termed a "non-metaphysical" interpretation of Hegel, which played an important role in the revival of interest in Hegel in academic philosophy during the second half of the century. Especially in North America, with important works by the close of the twentieth century, even within core logico-metaphysical areas of analytic philosophy, a number of individuals started to take Hegel seriously as a significant modern philosopher, although generally within analytic circles a favorable reassessment of Hegel was very distant.

Hegel's philosophy given in the "Preface" to his *Elements of the Philosophy of Right* captures a characteristic tension in his philosophical approach and his approach to the nature and limits of human cognition. "Philosophy," he says there, "is its own time raised to the level of thought." He felt contents of philosophical knowledge come from the historically changing events of contemporary culture, that there is the hint of such contents being "raised" to some higher level, presumably higher than other levels. Everyday experience, for example like that found in culture such as art and religion. This higher level takes the form of "thought," a type of cognition commonly taken as capable of having "eternal" contents as Plato believed.

Hegel's "metaphysical" view dominated much of the twentieth century, but has over the last few decades been contested by many Hegel scholars who have offered an alternative "post-Kantian" view of Hegel. Traditional "metaphysical" view of Hegel's philosophy is similar to Aristotle, in that "self evidence is the truth," and that everything is in a state of flux. Given the understanding of Hegel that predominated at the time of the birth of analytic philosophy together with the fact that early analytic philosophers were rebelling precisely against "Hegelianism." Hegel is seen as offering a metaphysico-religious view of God as the "Absolute Spirit," a "dogmatic" metaphysics against which Kant had rebelled. Understood in this way, Hegel is much more a pre- than post-Kantian thinker. Indeed, Hegel often seems to invoke imagery consistent with the types of neo-Platonic conceptions of the universe that had been common within Christian mysticism, especially in the German states, in the early modern period. The peculiarity of Hegel's form of idealism, on this account, lies in his idea that the mind of God becomes actual only because in our consciousness of God, we somehow serve to realize his own self-consciousness, and, thereby, his own perfection. Due to this and his concepts taken from its overtly religious content, it is hardly surprising that the philosophy of Hegel so understood is regarded as being very distant to the largely secular and "scientific" conceptions of philosophy that have been dominant in the modern world.

To many people Hegel had not only advocated a disastrous political conception of the state and the relation of its citizens to it, in his idea of the development of "spirit" in history, Hegel is seen as literalizing a way of talking about different cultures in terms of their "spirits," of constructing a nineteenth-century idea of historical progress.

The pantheistic legacy inherited by Hegel meant that he had no problem in considering an objective outer world beyond any particular subjective mind. Nevertheless, this objective world itself had to be understood as conceptually informed. It was objectified spirit. Thus in contrast to "subjective idealism" it became common to talk of Hegel as incorporating the "objective idealism" of views, especially common among German historians, in which social life and thought were understood in terms of the conceptual or "spiritual" structures that informed them. In contrast to both forms of idealism, Hegel, according to this reading, postulated a form of absolute idealism by including both subjective life and the objective cultural practices on which subjective life depended within the dynamics of the development of the self-consciousness and self-actualization of God, the "Absolute Spirit."

Hegel was still seen by many as an important precursor of other, more characteristically secular, strands of modern thought such as existentialism and Marxist materialism. Existentialists were thought of as taking the idea of the finitude and historical and cultural dependence of individual subjects from Hegel, and as leaving out all pretensions to the "absolute," in an atheistic slant, while Marxists were thought of as taking the historical dynamics of the Hegelian picture but reinterpreting this in materialist rather than idealist categories. As for understanding Hegel himself, the traditionally "metaphysical" view remained the dominant idea throughout the twentieth century. Existentialism we will examine later on. Hegel is cited as being a precursor to Heidegger, who was connected to the Nazis. On the contrary, Hegel insisted that Jews be treated as equals, that civil rights belonged to all men, regardless of ethnic background or religion. In fact, most Nazis disagreed with, if not publicly denounced Hegel. Indeed, almost all philosophy material was burned in great piles in the street, including with the formerly well read Plato in German schools. The ideas that remained became twisted, where by Nazi writers

186

were fond of citing parts of Plato's *Republic* and using it as basis for Fascist thought. Like most other aspects of Nordic traditions and paganism, many parts of Plato and Friedrich Nietzsche, and others were perverted.

However, while Kant had limited such conditions to "formal" structures of the mind, Hegel extended them to include aspects of historically and socially determined forms of embodied human existence. He felt history was not happy, but a tragic tale of possibility for us to learn from. Hegel agrees with Kant's diagnosis of internally contradictory nature of pure reason itself. His interpretation of the significance of this phenomenon is radically different to that given by Kant.

Again this works at a variety of levels - consider the attitude towards objectivity (which we'll see in Ayn Rand's ideas later) roughly correlating with "perception" in which the stability of the identity of some individual substance is made by making a distinction between the essential and accidental.

The *Encyclopedia of the Philosophical Sciences* is divided into three parts: Logic; a Philosophy of Nature; and a Philosophy of Spirit. This constitutes Hegel's philosophy of mind, the last, his philosophy of art, religion, and philosophy itself. The philosophy of objective spirit concerns the objective patterns of social interaction and the cultural institutions within which "spirit" is objectified. The book entitled *Elements of the Philosophy of Right*, which Hegel published as a textbook for his lectures at Berlin essentially corresponds to a more intense version of the section on what he called "Objective Spirit".

Hegel felt barter between two individuals involves an implicit act of recognition in each, in giving something to the other in exchange for what they want, and is thereby recognizing that other as a proprietor of that thing the value attaching to it, and Hegel's approach to punishment affords a good example of his use of the logic of what he called "negation." By punishing the criminal the state makes it clear to its members that it is the acknowledgment of right is expected social life - the significance of "acknowledging another's right."

We find, in Hegel's analysis that "civil society" is to be understood as dependent upon and in contrastive opposition with the more immediate form found in the institution of the family. This is the recognition rooted in both sentiment and the feeling of love, a one-sidedness that is the inverse of that found in market relations in which participants grasp themselves in the first instance as separate individuals who then enter into relationships that are external to them, such as the bonding needed by adoption.

Although most of Hegel's "mapping" of the categorical structures of the *Logic* onto the *Philosophy of Right* are far from clear to the layperson, the general idea is simple. Hegel's logic should be read as an attempt to provide an account of the conditions required for a well-developed self-consciousness. The most influential parts of Hegel's *Philosophy of Right* concerns his analysis of the contradictions found in an unfettered capitalist economy. On the one hand, Hegel thought that the interlinking of productive activities allowed by the modern market meant that "subjective selfishness" turned into a "contribution towards the satisfaction of the needs of everyone else." From a civil society, in which individuals are viewed in terms of the way they belong to the social body as a whole, Marx later used it as evidence of the need to abolish the individual propriety rights at the heart of "civil society" and socialize the means of production. Hegel did not agree with Marxism's idea of government in which everyone was equal, demanding that the State take charge of the populace. He felt that idea was an essential role within the state's capacity to provide the conditions for the existence - for rational and free-willing members of society. Rather, the economy was to be contained within a framework of the state, and its social effects offset by welfares state assistance, much like our own country today.

Immanuel Kant

Immanuel Kant was born in 1724 of East Prussia, studied at his hometown university, and worked there as a tutor and professor for more than forty years, never traveling more than fifty miles from home. Although, his outwardly, his life was one of calmness, his intellectual work easily justified the self-proclamation as having effected a major revolution in philosophy. Beginning with his thoughts on the difference between right- and left-handed orientations, Kant patiently worked out the most comprehensive and influential philosophical ideas of our era. Kant's view of the human mind is deceptively simple, but, like most philosophers, the details of its application are extremely complex. He held that the most interesting and useful varieties of human knowledge rely upon the mind and determines the conditions of its own experience. It is we, individually, that think all experience as scientific knowledge governed by traditional notions of reality. We apply reason to all possible experience, but regulative principles of this sort hold only for the tangible world as we know it. Kant felt since metaphysical propositions seek a truth beyond all tangible experience, they cannot be established within the bounds of reason.

His moral analysis of the operation of the human will, derived the necessity of a perfectly universalized moral law, and Kant grounded this conception of moral autonomy upon our concepts of God, freedom, and immortality.

Friedrich Wilhelm Nietzsche

Commonly referred to simply as Nietzsche, the German philosopher, born on October 15, 1844 was famous for his critiques of contemporary culture, religion, and philosophy centered on a basic question regarding the foundation of values and morality. Beyond the unique themes dealt with in his works, Nietzsche's powerful style and subtle approach are distinguishing features of his writings. Although largely overlooked during his short working life, which ended with a mental collapse at the age of 44, and frequently misunderstood and misrepresented thereafter, Nietzsche received recognition during the second half of the 20th century as a highly significant figure in modern philosophy. His influence was particularly noted throughout the 20th century by many existentialist, phenomenological and postmodern philosophers, including Anton LaVey, on concepts of Apollonian-Dionysian Duality, Eternal Recurrence, Will to Power, Nihilism, Herd Instinct, Ubermenschen, Attack on Christianity, and Master-Slave Morality.

He was most often criticized for his theories that modern man's actions thoroughly represent the rejection of God. Nietzsche despised and vehemently opposed Judeo-Christianity, not out of being blasphemous, but out of annoyance with such dogmatic thinking. LaVey led a movement across America that challenged complacency. Nietzsche described Christianity as a nihilistic religion because it evaded the challenge of finding meaning in earthly life. He felt it created a spiritual projection where mortality and suffering were removed instead of transcending into something superior - *in the here and now.*

Nietzsche's *Overman,* was an individual who can overcome the herd instinct, and who can take on values and morals not of the society they live in. Often his writings were full of hostility, fueled

191

by a hatred of mediocrity in humanity, reasoning that a day will come "when there will be a superhuman race, of superior qualities." Unlike the popular conception, Adolph Hitler took this idea, twisted and perverted it to mean kill anyone not Aryan. Instead, Nietzsche called for a race of smarter people, who realize humanity's full potential of creativity, intellect, and determination no matter their ethnic background. The *Ubermenvhen*, as Nietzsche called it, or "Overman" as it is in English, was in his mind the next step in evolution of humankind. Strength and ability are governed by mental resolve with a good dose of genetics thrown in. While Nietzsche's works did influence Adolph Hitler to some degree, it must be pointed out that "might" prevailing is a Nordic tradition, which is mirrored in many other cultures. In the 1930's ideals of Western culture were torn asunder by challenges that morality is subject to personal interpretation and Judeo-Christian beliefs in unconditional love and the meek/weak inheriting the earth. Many free thinkers who did not fall into the brainwashing of Hitler's fascist regime opposed those ideals and values.

What Nietzsche *actually* meant was a race of smarter people, those who realize humanities full potential of creativity, intellect, and determination. Could Hitler have been an overman, as he claimed? According to Nietzsche, this is most unlikely, given that rulers represent the moralities and ideologies of their time, as opposed to breaking free from them. In his famous text "*Tyrants of Democracy*", Nietzsche opposed the covert artist's overmen to the political leaders that Nietzsche despised, clearly anti-Nazism. Is not the concept of the Overman more limited to intellectual and artistic figures such as Goethe and Wagner? This seems far more likely, especially given that Nietzsche held Wagner and such people in very high esteem early in his life. Nietzsche believed that it was wrong to deprive people of their pain, because it was this very pain that stirred them to improve themselves, to grow and become stronger. It would overstate the matter to say that he disbelieved in helping people; but he was persuaded that too much Christian pity robbed people of necessary painful life experiences. Robbing a person of his necessary pain, for Nietzsche, was wrong. He once noted in his *Ecce Homo* "pain is *not* an objection to life."

According to Nietzsche, the Cartesian proofs for the existence of God are all examples of logic only a master from the nobility would invent. Thomas Aquinas's notions of what constitutes the "good life" is a particular example of what "good" might mean to a master. Nietzsche argues that Jesus transcended the moral influences of his time by creating his own set of values. As such, Jesus represents a step towards the overman. Ultimately, however, Nietzsche claims that, unlike the overman who embraces life, Jesus denied reality in favor of his "kingdom of God'. Jesus' steadfast refusal to defend himself, and his subsequent death, were logical consequences of his actions to create a self-fulfilling prophecy. Nietzsche criticizes the early Christians for turning Jesus into a martyr and his life into a story of the redemption of mankind in order to gain power over the masses, finding Christians to be cowardly, vulgar, and resentful. He argued that Christianity had become more and more corrupt, as successive generations further misunderstood and misinterpreted the life of Jesus. By the 19th century, Nietzsche concluded, Christianity had become so worldly that it became a parody of itself. It became a way of controlling the masses rather than a philosophy of love.

"Physiologists should think before putting down the instinct of self-preservation as the cardinal instinct of an organic being. A living thing seeks above all to discharge its strength – life itself is will to power; self preservation is the only one indirect and most frequent results."~ *Beyond Good and Evil, Friedrich Nietzche*

Nietzsche defined master morality as the morality of the strong-willed. For these men, the "good" as the noble, strong and powerful, while the "bad" are the weak, cowardly, timid and petty. He often referred to the common people who participated in mass movements and mass psychology as "the rabble." Valued above all else was, and still is, individualism particularly the opposition to pity and altruism. It is very clear that in their belief only certain individuals should attempt to break away from the herd mentality. Personally, I am a champion of individual struggle and self realization. I do not concern myself with mass movements or political parties that barter or quarrel for power. I recommend that those of us that are capable be aloof, overcoming the great nausea associated with nihilism that overcomes most others. Become the ship Nietzsche said that "sails over morality" and be the one who endlessly affirms your own existence. Initially we must become a destructive force, excising and annihilating the insidious "truths" of the herd, and reclaim the chaos from which pure creativity is formed. Destruction is not "evil". It is part of the natural cycle of life, as is creation. It is this creative existence that justifies suffering without displacing it in some fictitious "afterworld."

Martin Heidegger

Heidegger was a German philosopher born on September 26, 1889. He influenced many other major philosophers, and is regarded as a major or indispensable influence on existentialism, and postmodernism. He attempted to reorient Western philosophy away from metaphysical and epistemological and toward questions concerning the meaning of being, or what it means to be. Heidegger elaborated the writings of Friedrich Nietzsche. If Nietzsche was the thinker of objection against Judeo-Christianity, then Heidegger took his countrymen's thoughts to the next level, calling for a "willing of essence" in which man could gain it's collective needs and wants to shape a superhuman like society. Or rather as Hitler had the "Will" via superior force to cause change. Nietzsche was not a Nazi Party member, but later in life Heidegger was. It is clear that while he was associated with the Party, he did not agree with all of its ideals. The inhumanity or contempt for nobility did not bother him – it was more of a philosophical difference. He admired the Greeks, like Aristotle, who gave him inspiration to question 'truth' or our concept of it. Heidegger felt technology estranges us from Nature itself. Fascism does not acknowledge the freedom of the individual as does modern day Satanism, Existentialism, and Humanism. Total conformity is the key to Fascism – for Satanism it is more about survival of the fittest, in a Social Darwinist way of thinking. LaVey's Church of Satan is closer to Dashwood's aristocrats where self-indulgent was guided by commonsense, not as Hitler or Marx's overbearing style of governing. If anything, the reign of terror in the 1930's Germany was closer to the Vatican's rule during the Inquisition prior to the Renaissance.

Humanity needs freedom, creativity and personal expression, within sensible limitations. The chaos in Nietzsche's *God is Dead* saw society crumbling in our future as the weak became destroyed by its own idiocy and self-destruction. We are controlled more now by our media and government than by religion as our forefathers were. Peer pressure to fit in being the biggest culprit, and the "Herdist" thinking of popularity by doing the "in" thing. Hitler and other Fascist leaders (and Marx) felt the Herd Nietzsche spoke of demanded control or everything would collapse entirely, requiring strong leadership for the betterment of society. Most other modern philosophy differs, feeling stratification will cause the best to rise to the top, and act for its own betterment and the masses would see the example and follow suit. Hitler's men felt they were disciples of Nietzsche, and Heidegger was no exception. Heidegger's ideas were nearly fraternity like, with a militant collective mindset. Hitler's many leaders felt that the Knights versus the pious priests of the old days and the mentality of being nobles, who hunted, fought, and whose sexuality existed opposed to the humble, meek and pacifistic priestly class mirrored them. The guilt associated with man's carnal nature and the power of the Church over the commoner instilled a collective guilt over modern man. The German philosophers saw this as detrimental to the well being of society – possibly one reason for Hitler's inclusion of Asatru, as the warrior class was recreated. Nietzsche and Heidegger felt Christian notions like guilt were the root of the problem, and attacked the West with venom, citing morality as the enemy. They felt morality was absurd and outdated in question, Heidegger blazed a trail of challengers asserting, "Knowledge was a matter of process, not content, and the death of God rendered all truths as relative and subject to interpretation." He felt man needed to find his or her own moral truths without feeling absolutes in morals prior for two millennia, and questioning becomes the highest form of knowing. Truth need not be absolute; rather it was the act of challenging prior thinking that masqueraded as truth.

Although some of the thoughts of this period may have been sound, the extreme bigotry and manner of implementation were horrendous. One needn't subscribe to all aspects of a way of thinking that an individual conceptualized in order to appreciate the grains of truth they may contain.

Herbert Spencer

English philosopher and prominent liberal political theorist Herbert Spencer was born April 27, 1820. Although today he is chiefly remembered as the father of Social Darwinism, a school of thought that applied the evolutionist theory of survival of the fittest (a phrase coined by Spencer) to human societies, he also contributed to a wide range of subjects, including ethics, metaphysics, religion, politics, rhetoric, biology and psychology. He was a close contemporary of many famous philosophers and scientists of his period such as John Stuart Mill, Thomas Huxley and Charles Darwin and was renowned for the long-reaching, accessible, and profoundly sensible qualities of his work. Although he has often been criticized as a perfect example of scientism, he was at the time considered by many to be one of the most brilliant men of his generation. Herbert Spencer died on the 8th of December 1903.

Social Darwinism

Years after Darwin issued *Origin of the Species* and applied it to history and thought, added Darwinian concepts grew by the likes of Spencer, Mencken, and Anton LaVey. The concept of survival of the fittest was the idea of an animalistic king of the jungle attitude was mirrored in economics and lead a new school of thought among agnostic scholars. Ragnar Redbeard in, *Might is Right* wrote about much of this.

Might Is Right is written from the viewpoint that force always triumphs and a man has a duty to constantly protect, with continuation of force, what he has acquired by force *himself*. Laws are arbitrary constructs within which we have imprisoned ourselves; a real man makes his own laws! This 200-page essay on the righteousness of strength and social Darwinism was first published in 1896 and then later in 1910.

Promethean Flame by Corvis Nocturnum

This work, newly reprinted by Bugbee Books, outlines a case for "social Darwinism" that is one of the most brutal yet honest and most powerfully compelling I have ever seen. An excerpt from Redbeard, (whose true identity is never revealed,) follows: "He who saith unto himself, 'I must believe, I must not question' is not a man but a mere pusilanimous mental gelding. He who believes 'because it has been handed down' is a fool in his folly. Sagacious spirits doubt all things, and hold fast only to that which is demonstrably true....The rules in life are not to be found in Korans, Bibles, Decalogues and Constitutions, but rather the rules of decadence and death. The 'law of laws' is not written in Hebrew consonants or upon tables of brass and stone, but in every man's own heart. He who obeys any standard of right and wrong, but the one set up by his own conscience, betrays himself into the hands of his enemies, who are ever laying in wait to bind him to their millstones."

Certainly this did inspire countless anti-Semitic thoughts, and was a work favored by Neo-Nazi's but I hasten to say, stripped of its racial comments here and there, it contains much philosophy challenging our socially acceptable attitude that leave many at the mercy of our would be attackers – whether it be in the form of written, verbally, or by meekly accepting our fate in life due to conditioning. I am opposed to herd mentality as much as was Friedrich Nietzsche. This work opposes the blind thought that if it comes from America's history, in order to be patriotic, we must swallow it. Clearly, *Might is Right* has no appeal for those

199

sentimental totalitarians who profess "care" and "love" for humankind, and it is also clear, in the forward by The Church of Satan's founder Anton La Vey, how much of an influence it still has.

The author believes a strong man is the free man and "freemen should never regulate their conduct by the suggestion or dicta of others, for when they do they are no longer free." The free man is "above all laws, all constitutions, all theories of right and wrong. He supports and defends them, of course, so long as they suit his own end, but if they don't then he annihilates them by the easiest and most direct method." He also stated, "Liberty is honestly definable as a state of complete bodily and mental self-mastership...and thoroughgoing independence from all official coercion or restraint."

To be without property and unarmed is the condition of actual dependence and servitude. The results of laying down without a fight are countless in history, and although biased, the writer makes strong points for despising meekness. A case in point being explorers like Columbus and Cortez came to the "New World" bearing gifts. Their hosts were "blessed" with "gifts" like Small Pox, servitude, and genocide. As they convinced themselves they were "civilizing the savages," the European invaders dehumanized their "converts." Human beings became tools for empire building, or if they impeded imperial expansion, little more than insects to be exterminated.

Promethean Flame by Corvis Nocturnum

In the area of North America which eventually became the United States, one of the ultimate ironies occurred. Refugees from oppression in Western Europe became ruthless oppressors themselves. Victims became abusers as our ancestors nearly drove Native Americans to extinction. Might may not have been right in truth, but the Natives who fought are revered with honor, the passive dead forgotten. *Might is Right* points out that the rulers write the history books, proving that unarmed citizens are enslaved citizens, always have been and always will be. Crime is at its worst in the most law restricting gun areas of our country.

Although Redbeard seems to scorn moral codes, stating that "all arbitrary codes of right and wrong are insolent invasions of personal liberty" and that greatness lies "in being beyond and above all moral measurements," he is, nonetheless, a moralist. He makes plain his antagonism to Judeo-Christian morality, but his whole approach is constructed with a moralistic desire to redeem the human race from "evil." For him, what happens to be "natural" is "right" and the further human beings get away from "Nature," the further they depart from "right."

Might Is Right may be, as Anton LaVey mentioned, a work flawed by major contradictions. Like the Christian bible it can be used as a source for the most incompatible views, but indeed helps us to clear away not a few of the religious, moral and political superstitions bequeathed to us by our ancestors. Regardless of whomever Ragnar Redbeard was, and whatever criticisms may be leveled at his book, he remains worthy of the attention of all who are conscious that their "rights" are equal to their power.

Henry Louis Mencken

Better known as H. L. Mencken, twentieth century journalist, satirist and social critic, a cynic and a freethinker, known as the "Sage of Baltimore" and the "American Nietzsche". Born in September 12, 1880 Mencken is often regarded as one of the most influential American writers of the early 20th century. At one point in his career he was America's favorite pundit and literary critic at the same time. Mencken was an outspoken defender of freedom of conscience and civil rights, an opponent of persecution, injustice, Puritanism, and self-righteousness that masks the oppressive impulse. As a nationally syndicated columnist and author of numerous books, he is most remembered by assaulting America's preoccupation with fundamentalist Christianity. Mencken was a self-proclaimed elitist - elitism is a belief were a selected group of people whose abilities, specialized training, or other attributes place them above their fellow man. Thus elitists set themselves apart from the majority of people who do not match up with their abilities or attributes. Elitists traditionally value intellectualism, and an appreciation of classics, such as beauty in art, literature, and music. Also valued are wealth, power, and love of personal aesthetics. Instead of arguing that one group was superior to another, Mencken believed that every culture, regardless of race, gender, or sexual orientation, produced a few people of clear superiority.

Promethean Flame by Corvis Nocturnum
Ayn Rand

One of my own personal favorites among "new" philosophers is Ayn Rand. Born February 2, 1905 as Alissa Zinovievna Rosenbaum, she is best known for her philosophy of Objectivism and her novels *We the Living*, *Anthem*, *The Fountainhead*, and *Atlas Shrugged*. Her philosophy and her fiction both emphasize, above all, the concepts of individualism, rational egoism ("rational self-interest"), and capitalism, which she believed should be implemented fully via Laissez-faire capitalism. Her politics have been described as minarchism and libertarianism, though she never used the first term and highly detested the second. Rand felt Aristotle's "being qua being", the study of existence equally as important in today's world as in the past, the province of metaphysics. Ethics influenced her pondering, that the make up of a man is based on his character, reason, our values, and ability to reason. All the many things we are taught can be confusing – Rand said of man is equal to a computer- the output is equal to the input, and programmers are human and fallible. If we cannot refute something, how can we be certain we disagree with it?

Rand's novels were based upon the projection of the Randian hero, a man whose ability and independence causes conflict with the masses, but who perseveres nevertheless to achieve his values. Rand viewed this hero as the ideal, and the express goal of her fiction was to showcase such heroes.

Rand, who in essence, wrote that the concept of man was that of a "heroic being with his own happiness as the moral purpose of his life, with productive achievement as his noblest activity and reason as his only absolute." Her writings praised, above all, the human individual and the creative genius of which one is capable. She exalted what she saw as the heroic American values of egoism and individualism. Like LaVey, Rand also had a strong dislike for "occultniks"; charlatans who duped many into believing they had "psychic" powers. Both despised mainstream religions, as well as compulsory charity, all of which they believed helped foster a culture of resentment towards individual happiness and success. Religious and socially conservative thinkers have criticized Rand's atheism. Many adherents and practitioners of continental philosophy criticize The Church of Satan's celebration of rationality and self-interest. Whom else do we have to please but ourselves? Are we less important than other beings whom we rub elbows with? Hardly. Satanism may be selfish, but Magus LaVey was convinced that "good" is what we like, and "evil" is what we do not. Though she was hardly a hated personality of her day, Rand gave lectures to West Point Military Academy on March 6, 1974, and in doing so, advanced in America hope for the future via our accomplishments without fear of animosity from a pulpit on high. She addressed the graduates saying, "There is a special reason why you, the future leaders of the United States Army, need to be philosophically armed today. You are the target of a special attack by the Kantian-Hegelian-collective establishment that

204

dominates our cultural institutions." She felt the country was being weakened by disarming us intellectually and physically. She felt America was living proof against Kant's school of thought, that we have too much compassion for the weak, the inept. To her Objectivism was a tool to live on this Earth, that truth is the recognition of reality. She believed we as a society must push for the supremacy of the self, and our country by using reason.

Ayn Rand died March 6, 1982. A society based on her lives on in tribute to her, The Foundation for the New Intellectual, in a much similar fashion as does the Jungian Society.

Carl Gustav Jung

Born in July 26, 1875 the Swiss psychiatrist and founder of Analytical Psychology, Jung had a unique and broadly influential approach to psychology that strongly emphasized understanding the psyche through exploring the worlds of dreams, art, mythology, world religion and philosophy. Though not the first to analyze dreams, he has become perhaps the most well known pioneer in the field of dream analysis. Although he was a theoretical psychologist and practicing clinician for most of his life, much of his life's work was spent exploring other realms: Eastern vs. Western philosophy, alchemy, astrology, sociology, as well as literature and the arts. Jung also emphasized the importance of balance. He cautioned that modern humans rely too heavily on science and logic and would benefit from integrating spirituality and appreciation of the unconscious realm.

Interestingly, Jungian ideas are not typically included in curriculum of most major universities' psychology departments, but are occasionally explored in humanities departments.

Jung originally proposed many pioneering psychological concepts, such as the Archetypes and Collective subconscious.

Collective subconscious

The concept of group entities is not new. As mentioned before, Plato believed that transcendent forms exist from which the multitude of appearances come into our world. Jung psychology concluded that humans share one collective unconscious that lies deeper than the unconscious of each individual. He had observed a surprising similarity between deeply seated ideas of widely separated peoples. Similar basic concepts exist in the psyche of all of us, revealed by recurring dreams and subconscious ideas expressed spontaneously, without prior knowledge that others share them. Jung called these concepts "archetypes", which can be seen as the unconscious images of our instincts. Typical archetypes are "villain" and "hero" – we see this in the term "arch-villain". He stated, "To my mind it is a fatal mistake to regard the human psyche as a purely personal affair and to explain it exclusively from a personal point of view. Such a mode of explanation is only applicable to the individual in his ordinary everyday occupations and relationships" Sigmund Freud had voiced a similar opinion: "I have taken as the basis of my whole position the existence of a collective mind, in which mental processes occur just as they do in the mind of the individual . . ."

Promethean Flame by Corvis Nocturnum

Jung claimed that ancestral experiences accumulate as archetypes in the collective subconscious of humankind. Individuals "inherit" archetypal propensities much like Plato saw appearances in our world come from transcendent "eidos". Results showed invariably that people who have never been exposed to the correct versions can learn them much easier than the artificial equivalents.

Robert Luis Stevenson best presents this by deeply dramatizing the dual nature of man in *The Strange Case of Dr. Jekyll and Mr. Hyde*, a classic written in 1886. Having discovered the early draft of this story, his wife, horrified with what she read, hurled the ghastly manuscript into the fireplace. During a time of British technological advancement and leadership merging with the ideals of Western civilization, it was a commentary on living in a world of change outwardly as much as it was inwardly. Undaunted by his wife's prudish nature, and her fear of the realities of human nature he was attempting to express, Stevenson rewrote his classic of a scientist who discovers the unlocking of the mind's hidden duality of life. A concoction transforms the mild Dr. Jekyll into a purely evil acting and thinking individual uninhibited in his wants, pursuing "undignified pleasures", murder, and various other sins. The mixture to reverse this proves too weak, and Hyde takes control until he is found dead by suicide, leaving a full confession. This story seeks to have the reader sympathize with the traumatized victim who attempts to shake off responsibility for his actions, denying the evil in himself, something similar to split personalities.

These moral preaching classics attempt to lure the viewer into thinking that the struggle to gain knowledge and make use of powers that normal man cannot have (at least without selling their souls) is evil beyond redemption and the innocent 'victim' should be pitied. Consequences of disregarding morals leads one to tragic results – the dangers of acting as a sociopath, free of moral restraint, who they would have us believe needs be put down like a rabid dog. These so called monsters, or villains, clearly have left an impression on the collective subconscious of man over the ages due to the underlying reminders that we too are as they, Nietzscheian creatures staring back at us from the abyss. These archetypes relate to aspects we find disturbing in ourselves. It is easier to remove the unsettling taboo actions or wicked thoughts we all have and transpose it into such hideous caricatures. Fiction through the ages has been used to tell moral laden stories, wherein the villain, wearing black, was either hideous in appearance, by their deeds, or both. Yet we love them in spite of this or *maybe* more importantly, because of it. We root the underdog sympathetically most likely because silently we wish we *were* the creature who does what he wishes for vengeance, power, or wealth. Things we all wish for, to some degree or another, but rules of proper conduct prevent us from gaining. How we secretly hate it! We wish for the genie in the bottle, or for immortality. These figures offer that to us in escapism of books and in film.

Chapter Eight

A look back on yesterday

Perhaps out of all the many different aspects of the challengers described in *Promethean Flame*, it is the creative drive of the intellectuals that truly has paved the way forward. For it is out of the imagination of man alone that we find a way beyond our oppression. What one thinks and feels can never be extinguished. The past and future are what we envision it to be, it only takes courage to step forward and set the idea into motion and make it reality.

These remarkable challengers from esoteric orders and the occultist as well as philosophers outlined in this book well understood humanity's unshakable need for self-interest that continues to trickle down over centuries into a thundering evolution that has reshaped our very worldview.

Although the Masons' use of spirituality and perfection revolved more around the doing of the physical and connection to divinity, where the Rosicrucian were more into a connection of chemistry, both groups' primary goal was the advancement of science and faith without the dogmatic weight of The Church or various monarchies. Ironically, the pagans threw Christians to the lions, and Christians burned Pagans. Christian Pagan occultists

209

both had slaves in America while protesting servitude from their homelands. Philosophers have debated the need for any God or Gods, ranging from Deist to Atheist. People have always done that which was done to them, not learning the greatest mystery of mysteries might simply be "live and let live."

Nearly all, however, would be likely to agree that ritual is universal, and that no one particular path is identical, nor are the rituals of any one solitary performer. Rituals of nearly every indigenous tribe of peoples from times past to our present day Catholic Church are still used ritual in one form or another to establish a direct connection to the Divine Energy, God, or Gods.

A ritual, most simply put, is a performance meant to assist the outcome of the performer's desires, a dogmatic and anti-intellectual device. It is performed to disassociate oneself from the activities from the outside world while projecting one's will.

Psychodrama, as Anton LaVey called it, is the arousal needed to heighten a feeling inside oneself, combined with a symbolic representation. *The Encyclopedia of Witches and Witchcraft* written by Raven Grimassi calls rituals a "prescribed form of consciousness. All religions and spiritual, mystical and magical traditions have their own rituals, which are the means by which to contact the divine, or supernatural will, or forces helping the individual define him/herself in relation to the cosmos, and mark progress through life and spiritual unfolding."

The act of using magic or prayer is emotional rather than intellectual, for many would define magic as "the change in situations or events in accordance with one's will, which would, using normally accepted methods, be unchangeable." In ancient times, science was largely considered magic and blasphemy, yet is now accepted as obvious truth, not mad Dr. Frankenstein or Witches allied to the Devil.

By seeking out forbidden concepts in science, and expressing ourselves with passionate feeling in the arts, we expand our horizons. To sum up *Promethean Flame* I would paraphrase that the cycle of events begun by Aristotle fueling rational thinking and science greatly contributed to the wave of freethinkers who blended mystism, occultism, and early science. As far back as Hippocrates and worship of the God Hermes, healers, aboriginal shamans, and the ancient Druids who may have crossed paths with natives in what was to become America, we now have evolved to our current marvels in medicine most take for granted today. Even the early Masons, who were Christian influenced, were very strong proponents of science and mathematics in order to build the cathedrals of their day. They were the first to openly venture away from the strictly "because it's God's Will" opposed to the will of Man with the natural order of things, regardless of whether it is a multitheistic or self proclaimed 'godhead.'

From early Christian mysticism, Taoism, Buddhism, Cabbala, Sufism, Rosicrucian and the "Fourth Way", practical knowledge of both ancient and modern ethical and philosophical systems have advanced humanity to great heights.

Afterword

Over the recent years many things have become a given, the norm, such as a Goth kid walking the malls of America, and both Wicca and Satanism have become part of the Army Chaplin's guidebook, and most recently, the use of the pentacle of soldiers tombstones. In the eyes of those who lived before however, such things were undreamed of. We take for granted our luxuries in the here and now, yet now and then it is good to recall the struggle of those before us in order to appreciate how fortunate we are. It amazes me how so many will cry out over the treatment they get for being different when they should be satisfied in our day and age we can be as we wish and only get stares, instead of stoned. Not to say, however, such tragedies don't still occur. I have heard of a few sad incidents, such as a couple in the UK who were beaten by teenagers resulting in the death of one of the pair. Seeing that 'Goth' was included in the title, I surmised that the article was an anti-Goth protest, yet it turned out the couple was Goth and the attackers were preppie conformists! Closed minds still exist and we must be wary still, but keep a level head on your shoulders.

It is unfortunate that repression and the struggle for power over our fellow man cause so much strife and wanton destruction.

Nevertheless, perhaps without chaos we would not attempt to achieve order, thus continuing the cycle of all things. Perhaps the hodge podge theory of Hassan truly did make him the wise old man of the mountain. The wheel turns onward, and certain human beings who have and are yet to leave their mark on history will do so because they seek to climb higher, and reach beyond the goals of the average layman. For riches, sexual conquests, power, or for fame, these people aim for what others feel is unobtainable. We who share the spirit of Prometheus must refuse to be limited by the status quo. Instead, push aside limits in your search for knowledge and experience life with passion, as the great men and women did before you. Some of them paid the highest price of all, risking their very lives to pave the way.

I hope you have enjoyed your journey with me, discovering our long and winding road from Prometheus to our current times. It is my hope that I have inspired you to seek your own path. May you carry the torch onward for those who would seek the truth.

About the Author

Occult researcher and Gothic fantasy artist Corvis Nocturnum has owned an occult shop for several years while he maintained office as the Vice President of the Fort Wayne Pagan Alliance, a faith tolerance organization and acted as Vendor Director/Coordinator for Pagan Pride Day in Fort Wayne, Indiana. He has done lectures at various events all over Indiana, Ohio, and Illinois on the subjects in *Embracing the Darkness; Understanding Dark Subcultures,* work detailing the truth and crossover of alternative lifestyles, gaining the attention of readers all over the world. The grand and great-grandson of a Mason belongs to the Church of Satan, where he holds the title of Warlock. He remains involved in bringing about public awareness to Satanism's true nature at conventions and universities, by being an invited speaker at Indiana Purdue University's World Religions seminar. Various writings of his have appeared in newsletters and online groups, and he has spoken out on Dr. Ed Craft's online radio show, *Magick Mind Radio*. He is currently the co-publisher of Dark Moon Press and of The *Ninth Gate* magazine, a publication featuring fashion and interviews with bands in the Pagan, Satanic, Goth and Vampire communities. As well he is the manager of the psychical store of The Ninth Gate located in Fort Wayne, Indiana. Corvis enjoys painting and movies while not writing.

Corvis Nocturnum can be reached for questions and appearances at: Corvis@CorvisNocturnum.com or write via snail mail at: P.O. Box 11496, Fort Wayne, IN 46858.

Recommended Reading

<u>By Robert Greene</u>

The Death and Life of Philosophy, St. Augustine's Press (April 1, 1999)

The 48 Laws of Power, Penguin (September 1, 2000)

The Art of Seduction, Penguin; Reprint edition (October 7, 2003)

The 33 Strategies of War, Viking Adult (January 19, 2006)

<u>By Helen Ellerbe</u>

The Dark Side of Christian History, Morningstar Books (July 1, 1995)

<u>By Arkon Daraul</u>

A History of Secret Societies, Pocket Press (September 1962)

<u>By Charles Heckethorn</u>

The Secret Societies of All Ages and Countries, University Books (March 1966)

<u>By Micheal Howard</u>

The Occult Conspiracy, Destiny Books, (1989)

<u>By Peter LevenDa</u>

Unholy Alliance, A History of Nazi Involvement with the Occult, Avon Books (1995)

<u>By Lawrence Sutin</u>

Do What Thou Wilt, A Life of Aleister Crowley, St. Martin Griffin, (2000)

<u>By Partha Bose</u>

216

Promethean Flame by Corvis Nocturnum
Alexander the Great's Art of Strategy, Penguin (2003)

By Corliss Lamont
Philosophy of Humanism, Ungar Publishing, 01 January, 1974

By Tim C. Leedom
The Book Your Church Doesn't Want You to Read,
Truth Seeker; Reprint edition (September 1, 2001)

By Corvis Nocturnum
Embracing the Darkness; Understanding Dark Subcultures,
Dark Moon Press (May, 2005)
A Mirror Darkly, Dark Moon Press, (May 2006)

By Acharya S
The Christ Conspiracy: The Greatest Story Ever Sold. Adventures Unlimited
Press (September 1, 1999)

By Roger Shattuck
Forbidden Knowledge: From Prometheus to Pornography, Harvest Books;
Reprint edition (September 15, 1997)

By Voltaire
Voltaire - Candide Zadig and other selected stories. Introduction by John
Iverson. Signet Classics (2001)

By Niccolò Machiavelli
The Prince, Penguin Classics, 1998

Promethean Flame by Corvis Nocturnum

Schopenhauer Selections, Edited by DeWitt H. Parker, Charles Scriber's Sons (1928)

Religion Within the Limits of Reason Alone, Harper and Row (1960)

Florentine Histories, new translation. Introduction by Harvey Mansfield, Jr., Princeton University Press (August 3, 1990)

Discourses, Penguin Classics, 1984

The Art of War, Da Capo Press (September 4, 2001)

By Ayn Rand

Philosophy - who needs it, Signet Book (November, 1984)

Atlas Shrugged, Signet Book; 35th Anniversary edition (August 1996)

By Kurt F. Reinhardt

The Existententialist Revolt, The Bruce Publishing Company (1952)

By Friedrich Nietzsche

The Birth of Tragedy, 1872 in: 'Basic Writings of Nietzsche', trans. Walter Kaufmann, Modern Library, 2000

The Birth of Tragedy and the Case of Wagner', trans. Walter Kaufmann, Vintage, 1967

The Birth of Tragedy & the Genealogy of Morals, trans. Francis Golffing, Anchor Books, 1956

The Untimely Meditations, 1873-6, in *Unfashionable Observations*, trans. Richard T. Gray, Stanford University Press, 1998

Human, All Too Human, 1878, trans. R. J. HollingDale, Cambridge University Press, 1996

The Dawn, 1881, in: 'Daybreak', trans. R. J. HollingDale, Cambridge University Press, 1997

By Walter Kaufmann

Promethean Flame by Corvis Nocturnum

The Gay Science, 1882, 1887, trans. Walter Kaufmann, Vintage, 1974

Thus Spoke Zarathustra, 1883-5, in: 'The Portable Nietzsche', trans. Walter Kaufmann, Penguin, 1977

Beyond Good and Evil, 1886, in: 'Basic Writings of Nietzsche', trans. Walter Kaufmann, Modern Library, 2000

On the Genealogy of Morals, 1887, in: 'Basic Writings of Nietzsche', trans. Walter Kaufmann, Modern Library, 2000 and in: *The Birth of Tragedy & the Genealogy of Morals*, trans. Francis Golffing, Anchor Books, 1956

The Case of Wagner, 1888, in: 'Basic Writings of Nietzsche', trans. Walter Kaufmann, Modern Library, 2000

Twilight of the Idols, 1888, in: 'The Portable Nietzsche', trans. Walter Kaufmann, Penguin, 1977

The Antichrist, 1888, in: 'The Portable Nietzsche', trans. Walter Kaufmann, Penguin, 1977

Ecce Homo, 1888, in: 'Basic Writings of Nietzsche', trans. Walter Kaufmann, Modern Library, 2000

Nietzsche contra Wagner, 1888, in: 'The Portable Nietzsche', trans. Walter Kaufmann, Penguin, 1977

The Will to Power and Other Posthumous Collections, ed. and trans. Walter Kaufmann, Vintage, 1968.

Writings from the Late Notebooks, ed. Rüdiger Bittner, Cambridge University Press, 2003.

Philosophy and Truth: Selections from Nietzsche's Notebooks of the Early 1870s, ed. and trans. Daniel Breazeale, Prometheus Books, 1990.

Philosophy in the Tragic Age of the Greeks, trans. Marianne Cowan, Regnery Publishing, 1996.

The Pre-Platonic Philosophers, trans. Greg Whitlock, University of Illinois Press, 2001

From Shakespeare to Existentialism, Anchor Books (1960)

By Neil Schaeffer *The Marquis de Sade: A Life*

Dark Moon Press
P.O. Box 11496
Fort Wayne, IN 46858
www.darkmoonpress.com

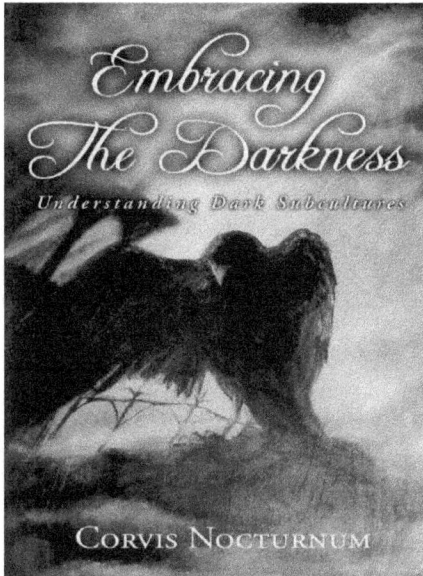

Embracing the Darkness
Understanding Dark Subcultures
By Corvis Nocturnum

The initial book of Dark Moon Press, written by Author Corvis Nocturnum, which brings you an unprecedented collection of Satanists, vampires, modern primitives, dark pagans, and gothic artists, all speaking to you in their own words. These are people who have taken something most others find frightening or destructive, and woven it into amazing acts of creativity and spiritual vision. Corvis himself is a dark artist and visionary, and so it is with the eye of a kindred spirit that he has sought these people out to share their stories with you.

$17.95 USD, 242 pages, paperback
Cover art by Corvis Nocturnum
Cover design by Monolith Graphics

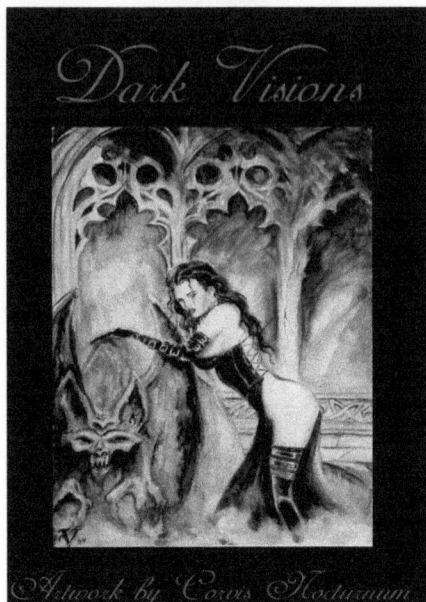

Dark Visions

Artwork by Corvis Nocturnum

Dark Visions is the first collection of artwork by Corvis Nocturnum spanning the last four years. Enter a world of breathtaking angels and seductive demoness, wicked fairies and mesmerizing vampires. With poetry, thoughts by the artist and an introduction written by artist Joseph Vargo.

$34.95 USD, 100 pages, paperback

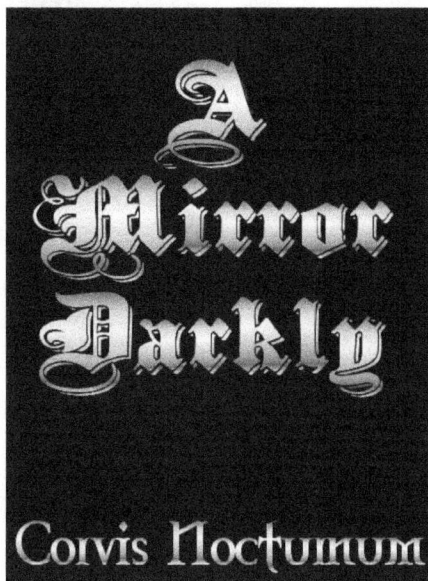

A Mirror Darkly

By Corvis Nocturnum

A collection of essays on society, philosophy and life in general written in the thought provoking way that only Corvis Nocturnum, author of the well received Embracing the Darkness; Understanding Dark Subcultures can, in this volume he brings you his personal collection of essays penned from years observing his fellow man. Few authors since Nietzsche or LaVey have so vehemently railed against societal, religious and governmental hypocrisies, laughable shortcomings and failings. Sharply critical of apathetic bottom feeders to being thoughtfully introspective, Corvis forces us to look at the creature that stares back at us from the abyss.

$16.95 USD, 152 pages, paperback

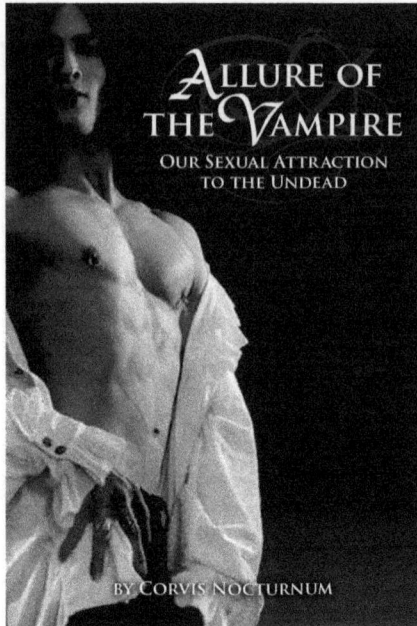

Allure of the Vampire

Our Sexual Attraction to the Undead

By Corvis Nocturnum

The mere mention of vampires used to be enough to make people think of a nocturnal predator. But over the centuries the vampire has changed from monstrous villain to sex object, for both men and women alike. Allure of the Vampire examines our intimate attraction to these beings in a detailed manner. Now, join occult author Corvis Nocturnum as he reveals the fascinating evolution of this icon as it has lured and enticed us in folklore, film and books from the days of ancient civilization to the living breathing inhabitants of our modern subculture of the vampire community.

$19.99 USD, 240 pages, paperback
Cover design by Monolith Graphics
August/September 2009

I, Lucifer

Exploring the Archetype and origins of the Devil

By Corvis Nocturnum

I, Lucifer challengers the idea that the Devil is a real being, and proposes that he is merely an archetype that has evolved from our collective unconscious, developed and reshaped constantly from barrowed ideas and given strength by sheer numbers of believers. It explores the myths and legends of not only Satan, but Lilith, fellow fallen angels, and the origin of Hell itself. Covering the vast perception of Satan from his origins to our modern day depictions in literature and film, this work also studies the impact in popular culture and in the public's impression as it evolved over the decades.

Tentative release date May 2010

These Haunted Dreams
By Michelle Belanger

Dark, sensuous, and lyrical, the supernatural fiction of author Michelle Belanger has enchanted the readers of Shadowdance, Necropolis, and Wicked Mystic since 1991. Now, collected for the first time, enjoy the chilling and erotic tales of vampires, demon lovers, and ghostly visitations in These Haunted Dreams. A visionary artist sees too deeply into the secret life of one of his models. A businessman obsessed with time runs late for work and changes his life forever. A new homeowner discovers that his beloved residence is alive and has no intention of letting him leave. And many more...

Cover art by Corvis Nocturnum.
$16.95 USD, 135 pages, paperback

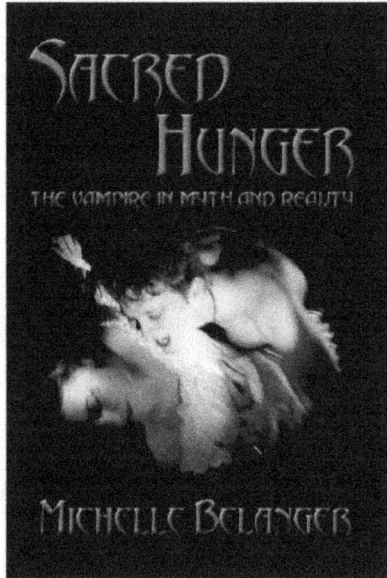

Sacred Hunger
By Michelle Belanger

Author Michelle Belanger has fascinated and informed readers about the vampire in folklore, fiction, and fact since the early 90s. Now enjoy all of Michelle's major essays on this fascinating topic, collected for the first time in one volume. Find out why author Bram Stoker wrote about vampires -- and what real-life psychic vampire inspired the figure of Dracula. Learn about the history and development of the modern community of real vampires. Explore the allure of the vampire in modern culture, and meet members of the vampire underground who have made this potent archetype a fundamental part of their lives...

$16.95 USD, 164 pages, paperback

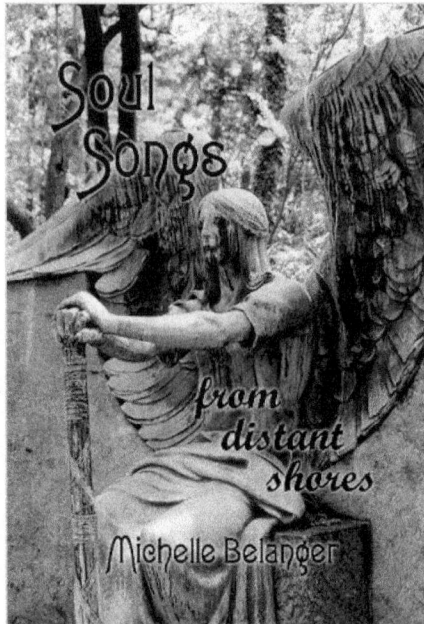

Souls Songs from distant shores
By Michelle Belanger

Exploring the poet in his varied guises as lover, mystic, lunatic, and seer, Michelle Belanger weaves lush and haunting images that will leave the reader awash in a sea of emotion. A collection as passionate as it is eloquent; Soul Songs takes readers through stages of elation, despair, inspiration, and consuming desire. Elegant, seductive, and insightful by turns, this rare collection of Michelle's poetry is not to be missed!

$12.00 USD, 52 pages, paperback

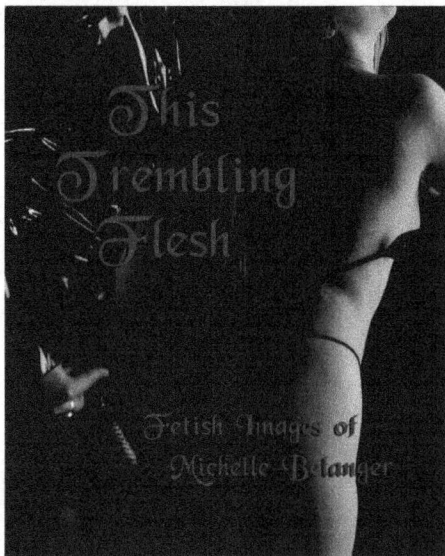

This Trembling Flesh
By Michelle Belanger

Get your fetish fix in style. "This Trembling Flesh" features over a hundred lush and sensual images in luxurious full -color. Featuring the modeling talents of author and vocalist Michelle Belanger with numerous guests, including the vampire Don Henrie.

$34.95 USD, 138 pages, paperback

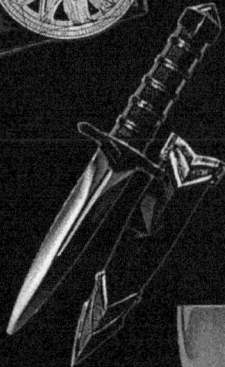

Promethean Flame by Corvis Nocturnum

Diabolic

Publications

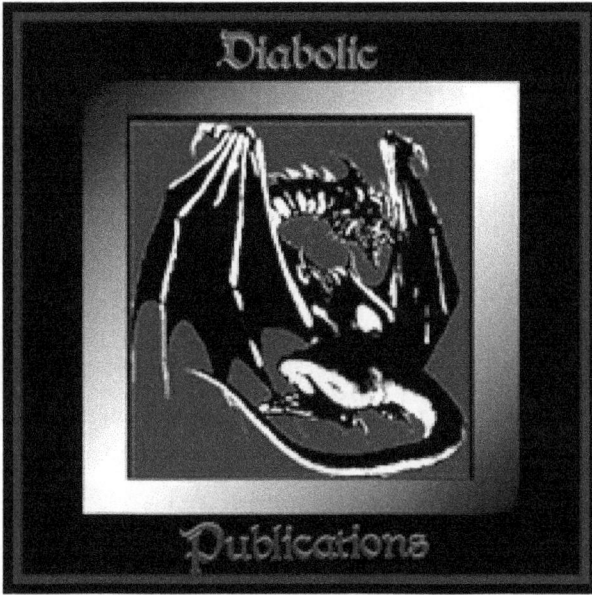

Diabolic Publications is a specialty publisher established in 2006 and is leading the way into the future with diverse genres of the dark, erotic and underground culture of today to appeal to the author and the reading public alike. We are a book publisher dedicated to producing the best in fiction and non-fiction works of quality. Our books are written by and appeal to the dark hidden nature of mankind. We publish the disturbing and controversial work of the most daring and innovative writers of our time.

Publishing trade and mass market paperback, as well as limited hardcover editions, **Diabolic Publications** seeks to bring some of the world's greatest stories to the mainstream audience. We are looking for highly motivated, talented and dedicated writers in the following genres.
(Fiction)
Dark Fantasy, Dark History, Erotic Horror, Gothic/Historic Horror (monster and physiological),
Magic Realism/Slipstream/Postmodern, Paranormal/Occult, Suspense/Thriller
Short story collections must be at least 150 pages and based in the genres listed, If you are submitting for inclusion in an anthology please query first with genre.
(Non-Fiction)
Unusual Art , Dark Paganism, Extreme Issues, Fringe/Underground Culture, Pop Culture,
Magic/Occult, Paranormal, Satanism, Vampirism

Query about our new imprint, **Of The Darkness Books**, taking hardcore Erotica, BDSM, and Fetish books to a new audience.

See our web site or myspace page for submission guidelines.

Contact us at:
www.diabolicpublications.com
contact@diabolicpublications.com
submissions@diabolicpublications.commyspace.com/diabolicpublications

231

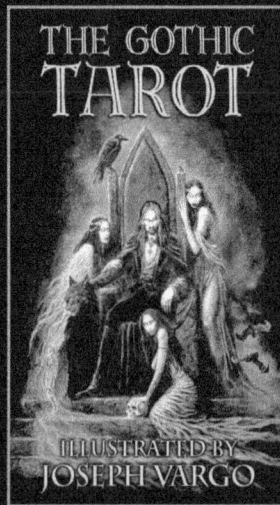

www.ingramcontent.com/pod-product-compliance
Lightning Source LLC
Chambersburg PA
CBHW031247090426
42742CB00007B/354